SPIRITUAL SLAVERY TO SPIRITUAL SONSHIP

SPIRITUAL SLAVERY TO SPIRITUAL SONSHIP

JACK FROST

Destiny Image® Publishers, Inc.
P.O. Box 310
Shippensburg, PA 17257-0310

*"Speaking to the Purposes of God for this Generation
and for the Generations to Come."*

For Worldwide Distribution, Printed in the U.S.A.

ISBN 10: 0-7684-2385-6

ISBN 13: 978-0-7684-2385-3

This book and all other Destiny Image, Revival Press, MercyPlace, Fresh Bread, Destiny Image Fiction, and Treasure House books are available at Christian bookstores and distributors worldwide.

For more information on foreign distributors, call
717-532-3040.

Or reach us on the Internet:
www.destinyimage.com

21 / 20

DEDICATION

With deep admiration, I dedicate this book to Captain Al Kline. He was the first man to believe in me when I did not believe in myself. When I was young, insecure, and seeking to find myself, Captain Kline not only took me into his heart and taught me the way of the sea, but he also became a warm and light-hearted father figure who imparted to me confidence, self-worth, and the belief that it is possible to overcome any adversity found at sea. These qualities have helped me to stay on course and remain afloat through many perilous storms in life.

ACKNOWLEDGMENTS

In the late 1990s, two teachers, who later became my friends, perhaps helped most in bringing me the revelation of living life as a son rather than as a slave or an orphan. James Jordan was the first person I heard teach on the orphan heart. You can learn more about him at www.fatherheart.net. The other was Mark Stibbe, from whose book, *From Orphans to Heirs*, I also received this revelation. My teaching on sonship would not have been possible without the contribution these men have played in my life in recent years.

In addition, three couples have contributed to the overall growth and development of my character as well as that of my wife's (Trisha), by standing with us as we worked out our unresolved father and mother issues on them. All the while, they saw the potential in our lives and patiently waited for us to grow up into mature sons and take responsibility for the mission that Jesus died for—living to experience God's love and give it away to the next person we meet.

I thank Bishop Houston and Evelyn Miles who have been my spiritual parents. They continued to love and value me during my years of spiritual immaturity when I valued the spiritual authorities in my life for what they could do for me and not for relationship.

It has been the gentle guidance of our friends and mentors, Roger and Pat Gosnell, who have helped to keep my vessel in deep waters when gale force winds nearly drove me aground. They did so by teaching me the way of humility and the willingness to go from a high place to a lower one in order to experience deeper dimensions of God's nature in my life. Roger taught me to never think myself too important that I would stop valuing cleaning the toilets. Commode ministry is the place where we truly find out what we are full of.

No telling what beach Trisha and I would have been stranded on if not for Major Richard and Christine Jones. These Salvation Army officers, like loving parents, nurtured us during our first few years as Christians and motivated us to fulfill God's calling. They encouraged me to leave the sea and discover new adventures, ministering to the broken and downtrodden.

TABLE OF CONTENTS

INTRODUCTION

Depending upon whom you might ask, I have been described as a man of great integrity, compassion, faithfulness, and sound character. But not many years ago, if you had asked my family, they would have probably used words such as intense, agitated, distant, driven, or obsessed. If you had inquired of someone in spiritual authority over my life, and they were painfully honest, they might have said, "Jack is self-centered, self-consuming, self-referential, or seeks to live for his own advantage by valuing people for what they can do for him and not for genuine relationship."

Outwardly, I was a person of service, sacrifice, self-discipline, and apparent loyalty. But inwardly, I was filled with spiritual ambition—the earnest desire for some achievement and distinction and the willingness to strive to achieve it. I had an insatiable desire to be seen and counted among the mature and successful. This resulted in a deep inner struggle with competition, rivalry, and jealousy, and left me with an ever pervading sense of restlessness—the feeling that there is something more that I have to do or put in order to feel valued, affirmed, accepted, or like I belong.

It was in the late 1990s when I began to realize that, even though I had been a dedicated Christian since 1980 and have had deep encounters with the Holy Spirit, my struggle was attributed to what I now know to be an orphan heart. I was raised with hyper-competitive athletic parents whose love did not cover me or give me a feeling of security and acceptance. To them I was not a "winner," so there was no place of affirmation, comfort, belonging, or affection. Therefore, I began to strive and wrangle for any recognition I could get, which led to a life of apparent success, but also a life of trying to hide feelings of frustration, agitation, and restlessness.

An orphan heart was not something I could cast out. Oh, how my wife tried though! Habit structures of thinking and ungodly beliefs had developed over a lifetime and had become orphan thinking. This had to be displaced by an experiential revelation of Father God's love and a repositioning of my heart toward sonship. Sonship is a heart that feels at rest and secure in God's love; it believes it belongs, it is free from shame and self-condemnation, it walks in honor toward all people, and it is willing to humble itself before man and God. It is subject to God's mission to experience His love and to give it away.

As movement from orphan thinking to sonship began in my life, some remarkable transformations started to occur. The heart of my rebellious children began to be restored to God's heart and my heart. My relationships with those in authority went from feeling like I had little favor to great honor being bestowed upon my wife and me. We also experienced an increase in the realm of finances and the ability to influence people's lives across the world for the Kingdom of God.

This book is designed to make my journey from slavery to sonship, your journey as well. I will lead you through numerous real-life experiences at sea, within my family, and within the church. Each story told will, to some degree or another, bring you to the point of thinking, That's me! I respond to people and circumstances in similar ways! I will not just reveal root problems, but I will give you practical truths that will help you begin movement from living life feeling more like a servant or slave to living life feeling like a treasured and favored son or daughter. You will be challenged and convicted, but also encouraged and comforted as hope for transformation and restoration helps you find safe harbor amidst the storm.

Experiencing Father's Embrace,

—Jack Frost

CHAPTER ONE

NO FEAR!

Mariners call it the "Sea of Fear."

Drake Passage, the 500 miles of southern ocean between Cape Horn and the Antarctic Peninsula, is home to some of the most dangerous waters on earth. Water temperatures there are so frigid that if you fall into the water, you will become unconscious from hypothermia in less than five minutes—with death quickly following. It is also the most confusing body of water in the world to navigate. With no continent to block it, the water in Drake Passage swirls continuously in a circulatory motion from west to east. Add in winds that blow in excess of 35 knots for over 200 days a year, and you have an ocean passage that is dangerously unpredictable. Conditions can change from calm to stormy in a heartbeat, and you never know from what angle the waves will come at you. The Sea of Fear has been the watery grave of over 400 boats and ships that have gone down with all hands.

As a licensed fishing boat captain and more than a bit of an adventurer, I get my kicks from traveling into the remotest regions of the earth. That is how I ended up recently as part of an expedition sailing from the southern part of Chile, past Cape Horn and into the Sea of Fear. Believe me, it was quite a ride, guiding a 74-foot sailboat on a 3-day journey through 40- to 50-knot winds with seas up to 30 feet! We then spent a couple of weeks in Antarctica. It was the time of year on the southern continent when the sun never drops below the horizon. For two weeks we saw no darkness.

As we began our return trip through Drake Passage, the captain of the expedition, who has had years of experience sailing in this part of the world, said, "This is the calmest I have ever seen the Sea of Fear." And, indeed, there was very little wind—so little wind, in fact, that we were operating on motor power. At the same time, we had put out every square foot of canvas possible trying to catch any wind we could.

We were 150 miles south of Cape Horn in a region of the sea where many boats have gone down due to 10,000 feet of water constantly moving with the current that comes up the continental shelf and kind of explodes into the air. This was perhaps the most treacherous part of the passage.

It was 1:30 in the morning and we were experiencing the first darkness in two weeks, but only for an hour. Then the sun would rise again.

Of the eight of us on the expedition, five were in their bunks below, while the captain, a successful Christian artist friend of mine named David Costello (www.davidcostello.com), and I were on duty in the wheelhouse. The night had been rather uneventful with no wind and relatively calm seas; and we were there mainly just to work the sails and perform other routine tasks as needed. The heated wheelhouse was warm and cozy. Outside, however, the temperature was in the 30s, which actually was somewhat warm for that time of year.

Holding On

Suddenly, with no warning, the wind rose sharply. Icy sleet blew sideways as the wind quickly reached gale force velocity, and in a matter of minutes the temperature dropped to well below freezing. With every square foot of sail out, we immediately faced a dangerous situation. The sudden onset of gale force winds hitting that amount of canvas threatened to tear the mast off and capsize our vessel. The list meter, which tells how far to port or starboard a boat is leaning, and which pegs out at 45 degrees, was locked on the peg as the wind in our sails keeled us over so far to starboard that water was washing up on the decks.

The captain screamed at us, "Out on deck! We've got to take in some canvas or we may lose the mast!"

It was at this point when we experienced the first real moment of panic during the entire trip. Here was a man who knew Antarctic travel and southern ocean sailing, and who had sailed around the world a number of times, and *he* was anxiously scream- ing at the two guys who didn't know a thing about the southern ocean or this type of sea. So naturally, we were fright- ened...*terrified* is a better word!

There was no time to don our arctic gear (masks, suits, and gloves) because every second lost would increase the chance of disaster. But as we ran toward the door, the captain shouted, "Get your harnesses on!" These harnesses had a 10-foot length of rope or lifeline that snapped to another rope that ran from the stern of the vessel to the bow. Wearing a harness ensured that we would remain lashed to the boat in the event we were washed overboard, making it possible for us to be hauled in again (provided, of course, that we didn't have a heart attack from going over the side in a storm or that hypothermia didn't claim us first)!

With our harnesses on, we flew out the wheelhouse door and onto the deck. Instantly, the wind-blown sleet felt like hundreds of needles piercing our unprotected skin. The captain took amidships to take in the mainsail and assigned me to the starboard side where one of the other sails was secured. Because we were listing so heavily, the water was about knee-deep at my location, and the only thing that kept me inside on the deck were two steel cables running along the side of the boat.

Except for this one trip, David had never been in open ocean for any major length of time. So, as he told me later, he became panic-stricken as he headed up to the bow where the captain had ordered him to go. If you are ever on the bow when the seas are running high, you will get the ride of your life! Even when there is no wind in the Sea of Fear, you can still experience 10-foot swells because of the motion of the water in that area. And when the wind comes up, it turns immediately into 20- and 30-foot seas. As the bow rises up into the heavens, inertia glues you to the deck. But as the boat crests the wave and falls into the trough, the bow drops from under you, suspending you suddenly 1 or 2 feet above the deck until it comes back up to meet you at the start of the next wave. And the whole time you're grabbing hold of anything you can so as not to be washed overboard.

Meanwhile, I was on my hands and knees crawling out to the starboard side to take in enough canvas to keep the mast from being ripped off. The wind was howling, the sails were snapping, and the freezing spray and blowing ice were numbing me to the bone. Finally, I finished the job as the captain completed his, and he yelled, "Get back in the wheelhouse!"

As soon as the captain and I crawled back into the luxurious warmth of that wheelhouse, I said, "Man, what an adventure! That was awesome! That's the kind of thing I came on this trip for!" Then we looked up through the windshield and discovered that David was still on the bow! He had brought his sail line in, but in doing so had piled all the extra rope on top of the lifeline that attached his harness to the rope leading from bow to stern. Although he seemed to be tangled, he was still able to move, yet David was frozen on the bow. He remained on his knees, gripping the wire railing for all he was worth, and every time the bow dropped, he lifted 1 to 2 feet off the deck, depending on the size of the wave. Icy sleet was blowing sideways, he was without his arctic gear, his hands were frozen and numb, and he seemed paralyzed.

The captain and I were sitting in the warmth of that wheelhouse wondering, *What is he doing?* We just couldn't figure out why David didn't come in. Finally, we decided, "Maybe he's just enjoying the ride of his life." A few minutes later, David finally crawled his way back to the wheelhouse. "Dave, what were you doing out there?" He didn't say a word. He just went below and into the head (bathroom), and didn't come out until 15 minutes later.

Letting Go

For the next several days David didn't say a word to any of us about his experience on the bow. Whenever we brought the subject up, he just said, "I can't talk about it." Finally, when we were at the airport for six hours, waiting for our flight home, David began to open up.

"David," I said, "tell me what happened to you."

He said, "I had my 'Shackleton moment.' I had the moment that I came with you on this crazy trip to Antarctica for."

Sir Ernest Shackleton was the leader of an expedition to Antarctica in 1915-17 who, along with his entire crew of 27 men, survived for two years on the southern continent after their ship, the *Endurance*, had its hull crushed by pack ice.

David was now 58 years old. He had grown up under an extremely harsh home situation; and until his mid-30s, he had been an alcoholic. Along the way he had wounded the lives of his wife and daughters, and his own life had come apart at the seams.

Then David had a deep encounter with Jesus Christ and with the Holy Spirit. After he became a Christian, he began following after the "Father's heart" message that I teach through Shiloh Place Ministries. That's how I came to know him. He attended many of our events, and because he loved the sea, we easily became good friends.

In the meantime, David developed a passionate desire to see his family healed and restored but became very frustrated with himself. "I just can't get it," he once confessed to me. "I receive all these teachings, but the love of God just won't move from my head to my heart. My family still has so much more healing to go through. And I know I've got to have a breakthrough in my fear of intimacy in order to help facilitate healing with them. It's like I'm in 'numb-numb-ville.' I know all the principles of the Bible. I know the principles of God's love, but it has never become truly *real* to me."

That day in the airport, David said, "When I was on the bow, I couldn't get my lifeline untangled. I knew I was stuck. My only possibility of getting free was to unsnap the lifeline from the safety rope and make my way back into the warmth of that cabin without it. But the fear of being washed overboard hindered me from letting go. And I sat there thinking, *This isn't too bad of a way to die.*" (Hypothermia gives you a cocaine-like buzz just before you go under.)

"I was just getting to the buzz part," David said, "which I hadn't had in about ten years, and was even beginning to enjoy it. That's when I heard a voice inside me say, 'Live!' Then I heard it again: 'Live!' And then a third time: 'Live!' And I said, 'Father, is that You?' And He said, 'It's time to let go of the pain of your past and begin to live for the restoration of your family. Just let go.' I thought, *I can't end it here without the hearts of my family being restored.* That's when I unsnapped my lifeline."

David confronted his fears and chose life. He risked letting go in order to bring healing and restoration to those whom he had inflicted the most pain upon in the years before he found the Lord.

As David told me later, when he unsnapped his lifeline, he sat and waited until he bottomed out in the trough between two waves. Just as the bow started to rise back up, when inertia held him to the deck, he jumped back toward the stern, seeking to crawl out of his entanglement. Fortunately, his lifeline pulled free of the snaky pile of rope that was on top of it. He began crawling his way along the deck, which was not canted over as far to starboard as earlier because we now had less sail out. Safely clear of the entangling rope, David reattached his lifeline farther back. Finally, he crawled into the wheelhouse, soaked and shivering, and disappeared into the head below. I assumed he was going to change his pants. I was wrong.

"Jack," he later told me, "when I went into the head, I curled up in a ball like a little boy. For 15 minutes I was curled up in a fetal position. It finally happened! Everything you've been preaching on and I have been listening to for eight years finally happened! I was a little bitty boy in the arms of a great big Daddy! As I was lying there weeping in the arms of Father God, the 'numb-numb-ville' of my emotions began to fade away, and I knew I was going home a different man!"

Recently I talked to Dave and asked him, "Dave, do you still have it?"

"I don't *feel* any different," he answered, "but people *tell* me I'm different. Everybody asks me, 'What has happened to you?' Even my wife and children are saying, 'You're not the same person you were.' I don't feel any different, but they say that life is flowing out of me now."

After years of being afraid to trust, afraid to open up even to the ones he loved, and afraid of being rejected, David experienced the defining moment of his life on the bow of a storm-tossed sailboat in the middle of the night. David confronted his fears in the Sea of Fear…and chose *life*.

Fear…or Father's Embrace?

What would *your* life be like if you had no fear?

What if you had no fear of man? No fear of what others think about you because you are secure in the love of your heavenly Father and in His kind thoughts toward you? No fear of opening your heart to truly experience the depth of God's love so that you could live and give away that love to the next person you meet? What would your life be like if you had no fear?

What would your marriage be like? What would your family life be like? Your other relationships? What if you were not afraid to trust, to become vulnerable, to reach out and touch others, and to let them touch you? Fear paralyzes us. Like David, frozen on the bow of that sailboat, mere yards from the safety of the wheelhouse, fear can stop us from making choices that will bring us warmth, security, and abundant life full of love, peace, and tenderness.

What would your church be like if you had no fear? What if everyone in your local body of believers was set free of the fear of trusting, the fear of rejection or abandonment, and the fear of opening their hearts to love and intimacy? Fear disables us. We can know all about the things of God and yet our fear of trusting and of intimacy can hold us back from receiving the benefits of what Jesus died for—to bring restoration and healing in our families and our relationships. So many of us Christians do all the right Christian "stuff," yet fear continues to hold us back from casting ourselves fully into our loving Father's embrace.

Do you rise up every morning feeling like a son or daughter secure and confident in your Father's love, and living to give that love to others? Or do you get up every day feeling like a slave, struggling constantly with fears of failure or rejection, unable to trust, and wondering what you have to do to appease the Master today? Moving from slavery to sonship or daughtership is a matter of reaching the place where you get up in the morning feeling so loved and accepted in your Father's heart that your whole purpose for existence becomes looking for ways to give that love away to the next person you meet.

What would your life be like if you had no fear?

We either live our life as if we have a home, or we live our life is if we don't have a home.[1] We either live our life feeling safe, secure and at rest in Father's heart, experiencing His love and giving it away, or we live our life with apprehension and uncertainty, struggling constantly with the fear of trusting, the fear of rejection, and the fear of opening up our heart to love—the three fears common to all people.

So many of us have hooked our lifeline (sense of security) into "counterfeit affections," that sooner or later will entangle us in unrealized hopes and unfulfilled dreams. Instead of drawing our energy and our source of life and peace from the love of God, we try to find them in these counterfeit affections of performance, the passions of the flesh, power and control issues, possessions, position, people, or places. Somehow we think that unless we have these sources of comfort in our lives, we simply can't go on.

Let's be honest—we all have counterfeit sources of comfort, don't we? Every one of us has people or possessions we turn to or attitudes or behaviors we fall back on when life does not go the way we want it to. Counterfeit affections exert a strong pull, even when we realize they are counterfeit. Sometimes it is easier to hold onto the familiar, and make it our lifeline even if it does not satisfy, than to risk letting go in order to grab hold of something else that will. When you're out on the bow being tossed by every 20-foot wave and with sleet whipping against your face, it's easy just to grab hold of whatever you can find and say, "I'll just ride it out right here." But unless you let go—unless you relinquish your grip on your false sense of security and comfort—you may never attain the true warmth and security of the wheelhouse—Father's embrace.

For those 21 days that we were in Antarctica and traversing Drake Passage, that cramped cabin was home. Whenever we were there, we were warm, safe, and sheltered from the wind and the waves. The problem with us today is that so many Christians have never made their way beyond the sea of fear into a place of safety and security. Isn't the brokenness of so many of our marriages, families, and other relationships evidence enough?

Living life as if we have a home means living to experience God's love on a continuing and ongoing basis and making that love known to others. As Christians, we are sons and daughters of God, yet so many of us live as if we don't have a home. We live, think, and act like fatherless orphans because we have never truly embraced Father God's love on a personal level. The storms, setbacks, and disappointments of life have made us afraid to trust, afraid to let go, afraid to risk becoming vulnerable by believing God when He says, "I love *you*." Because we do not love ourselves, we feel unlovable and find it difficult if not impossible to believe that anyone else could love us, including God. The thought of Him loving us personally seems too good to be true...and much more than we deserve.

And that's precisely the point: It *is* much more than we deserve. But it is also true. God Himself said, "*I have loved you with an everlasting love; I have drawn you with loving-kindness*" (Jer. 31:3b). Take that verse personally because God means it personally. God never created you to be an orphan with no home. He created you to be a beloved son or daughter who has found a home in His embrace.

We Have a Home

In fact, all of creation is about God wanting to make His home in you and, indeed, in all of us. And He will not rest until He accomplishes it. Isaiah 66:1 says, "*This is what the Lord says: 'Heaven is My throne, and the earth is My footstool. Where is the house you will build for Me? Where will My resting place be?'*" Not in a temple or anyplace else that is built by the hand of man. Revelation 21:3 provides the answer: "*And I heard a loud voice from the throne saying, 'Now the dwelling of God is with men, and He will live with them. They will be His people, and God Himself will be with them and be their God.'*"

God is saying, "I will not leave you like an orphan. You have a home with Me." Home is a place of safety and security. It is a place of warmth and love. If you're having a "bad hair day" and everybody is coming against you at school or at work and nobody is speaking anything good about you, home is the place where you can go and hear the voice of your Father say, "No matter what anybody else says, you are the child I love and on whom My favor rests." Home is where you constantly hear the voice of God speaking His affirmation over you, His love over you, and His forgiveness, compassion, and grace over you.

Without this deep experiential knowledge and understanding of Father's love and that you have a home in Him, it becomes so easy to live your life as if you don't have a home, which is a life of fear. And fear produces "numb-numb-ville." It makes you unable to healthily connect emotionally with God or anyone else with whom you have a relationship. Living like an orphan means struggling constantly with the fear of trusting. It is a life of independence where you believe you are completely on your own. It means living in a state of agitated resistance against people who do not think like you. When you live your life is if you don't have a home, you see every person—even loved ones—as a potential threat or enemy to your independence.

Whether you live your life as if you have a home or live your life as if you don't have a home depends on how you think God feels about you. If you believe that God loves you just as you are, you will live life like a son or daughter of the King. If, however, you believe that God is mad at you and that you always have to try to find out how to appease Him, you will live like an orphan. This is an important distinction because however you think God feels about you is the way you will treat others in your everyday relationships.

All of creation begins and ends with the Father longing for relationship with you as His beloved child. He created you to live your life as if you have a home. Did you get up this morning and hear the loving voice of your Father say, "Don't worry that you don't have everything together; that's OK. I don't expect you to get it perfect. I love you so much just the way you are. You are the son/daughter I love and in whom I am well pleased"?

Or did you get up thinking, *Nobody loves me. Nobody cares about me. I've got to have devotions today, and pray enough, and get my three Bible chapters a day in, and do all the right Christian stuff, just so I can get a crumb from the Master's table today?* You will treat yourself and others according to the way you think God feels about you. If you know you are loved unconditionally, you will love yourself and others with that same kind of love. But if you feel you have to perform in order to be of value to God, then you will portray the thought to others that they need to perform in order to be of value to you. Either you live your life as if you have a home, or you live your life as if you don't have a home. Fear...or Father's embrace!

Come Home

I am convinced that in this season of church history more than any other since the days of the apostles, God is calling us to experience a homecoming. He is calling us off the sea of fear into a calm harbor of refuge and safety. It's hard to beat the feeling of exhilaration you get when you move from a place of not knowing whether you will be alive or dead in the next minute into the warmth of that wheelhouse. During that stormy night on Drake Passage, something came alive inside both David and me. He said, "I don't even know what it was, but I know I encountered God in a deeper way than ever before."

That's what happens when you find yourself frozen on the bow in the sea of fear. You never know what's going to happen next. But when you choose to confront the sea of fear and cast yourself in faith into the arms of a loving Father, you begin to discover the purpose and meaning of life. As He did with David on the bow of that sailboat, God is saying to you, "Live! Live! Live!"

God is saying to all of us: "Come home." And where is home? Anywhere He is. We hear a lot about the Kingdom of God in our churches these days; to me, the Kingdom of God means seeing God's will and purpose come to pass on earth as they are in Heaven. Whenever I think about the Kingdom of God, I always refer back to a few verses in the Gospel of John. *"The Word became flesh and made His dwelling among us. We have seen His glory, the glory of the One and Only, who came from the Father, full of grace and truth"* (John 1:14). Jesus came from the bosom of the Father. The original Greek says that He came "from the Father's heart." And the heart of the Father is where He invites us to return. That is our home.

Jesus says in John 8:14, *"I know where I came from and where I am going."* He will return to the place from which He came, and He wants us to be with Him: *"In My Father's house are many rooms; if it were not so, I would have told you. I am going there to prepare a place for you. And if I go and prepare a place for you, I will come back and take you to be with Me that you also may be where I am"* (John 14:2-3). Jesus is saying to us, "I'm fixing up a special place for you in the family dwelling. My Father's house will not be an empty house. It is your home in His embrace."

Christ, who created all things, came from the bosom of the Father, a place of warmth, safety, and security. He came to make it possible for His home to become our home so that we will know that we are not orphans. Subsequently, when crisis comes, we can be confident that we do not have to face it alone because Father is always there.

No one goes through life without experiencing some degree of shame, disappointment, or betrayal. When these and other crises come, where do you hook your lifeline? That is what creation is all about—God making His home among humankind. It is about knowing we have a Father and a home. And isn't that what we all are looking for? God created every human being to be a son or daughter to someone. All creation began with the Father desiring relationships with sons and daughters.

Frozen in "Numb-Numb-Ville"

Until about ten years ago, I was an intense, authoritarian, and performance-oriented husband and father. I was radically born again in 1980 but for the next 15 years still thought and lived like an orphan because I never really understood the depth of the

Father's love for me. I thought I had to perform and strive to earn it. Consequently, my orphan heart negatively affected every relationship I had, particularly with my family. Finally, God transformed my heart, and I learned to relinquish my orphanhood and embrace sonship. My transformation was both sudden and dramatic. My wife says that God changed me more in 45 minutes than I had changed in my entire previous 15 years of walking with Him. I wrote about this experience in my first book, *Experiencing Father's Embrace*.

My daughter was 14 at the time. Suddenly, I went from an agitated dad to a compassionate father—a change that literally melted her heart. I had been so hard to live with that she had reached the point of wishing that whenever I left the house to go on a ministry trip, I simply would not return. She said that prior to my receiving a revelation of God's love, whenever I was home there was no joy in the house; there was only fear—fear of trusting, fear of rejection, and fear of opening her heart to love. Embracing Father's love made all the difference. In a matter of months, my relationship with Sarah changed from an almost total lack of tenderness, affection, and warmth to the place where she became "Daddy's girl."

From the time she was 14 until she was 17, Sarah and I enjoyed the kind of relationship any father and daughter would long for. She would run in the house and yell, "Dad, where are you?" Then she would jump on my lap, give me a kiss, and tell me what an awesome and wonderful dad I was.

One day when she was 17, I was driving her to school and I said, teary-eyed, "Sarah, I just love you so much!"

"Daddy," she replied, "would you quit before my makeup runs?"

It was a very tender moment between us. Later that day as I was watching the news and my wife, Trisha, was fixing dinner, Sarah arrived home from school. She came through the back door, slammed it, blew right by her mom without a word, blew right by me without a word, and went straight up to her room. I then heard the bedroom door slam behind her.

Trisha looked at me and said, "What did you do to her this morning?"

"I didn't do anything," I replied. "Everything was great!"

"Well, you'd better go find out what's wrong."

I knocked on Sarah's door. "Is everything all right, Sarah?"

"Yes!"

"Did I do something wrong?"

"No!"

"Well then, why don't you come out and tell us about your day?"

"I don't want to!"

(Every parent of a teenager recognizes this tone and dialogue!)

A little while later, I called Sarah for supper.

"Do I have to come?"

"Yes, you have to come."

She came to the table, sat in the chair with her arms crossed, and just glared the whole time. She ate nothing. After supper she went back to her room and locked the door. This isolation went on for weeks.

What hurt so much was that if I had known what I had done wrong, I would have tried to make it right, but I couldn't think of anything I had done, and neither could Trisha. As the days went by, we began to watch Sarah become more and more consumed by fear. Her hands started shaking. She couldn't look us in the eye. And whenever it was time to go to church, she pitched a fit: "I don't want to go!" For some reason we could not fathom, Sarah had abandoned the warmth and security of the wheelhouse and was now "on the bow," frozen in "numb-numb-ville."

Finally, after several weeks, Sarah began opening up to her mother. She had started trying to stand up for righteousness at school regarding some things that were happening with some other Christian girls. Unfortunately, they responded by trashing her. The same thing happened at church. Now all her friends had pushed her to the outside looking in, and she didn't know how to get back inside. I would drive her to school, and she would be desperately trying to hold back the tears, not wanting to go because of the way other people were treating her on a daily basis.

Trisha tried to encourage her. "Go talk to your dad. People come from all over the world to hear him. You have free access to him any time. Talk to him."

"I don't want to talk him! I don't want to talk to anybody. I want everybody just to leave me alone!"

Learning the Father's Heart

One night I stayed up all night praying because my heart was so burdened for her. I knew that if she, like anyone else, would continue to close her heart off to love, she would most likely find comfort somewhere else. The enemy is very good at sending the wrong people to us just at our time of greatest crisis. Whenever you cut yourself off from those people who love and care about you, get ready for the enemy to entice you with a counterfeit affection that you think is an answer for the need in your life.

I prayed for Sarah all night: "Please, God, help her find her way home. She's living her life as if she doesn't have a home. Help her find her way back to You."

The next morning as I was driving her to school, she noticed that my eyes were all puffy.

"Dad, you look terrible!"

"Well, I've been up all night."

"Are you and Mom having problems right now?"

"No, I've been up all night because my heart is breaking for you. It's been weeks since you've come in the house and sat in my lap and given me a hug."

Sarah shot me the look that said, "Don't go there!" But I still had five more minutes of driving time before we arrived at the school. She was a captive audience. "Sarah," I said, "my heart is breaking because everything in me experiences such great joy when I know that life is going well with you. And I see that your world is collapsing, and I know that what you need more than anything else is to hear me say, 'No matter what's going on, Sarah, I love you the way you are. And you are beautiful in my eyes.' All I want is a hug."

I believe that in those few hours during the night, I learned what it means to grieve the Holy Spirit. It has to do with a loving Father witnessing the pain that we, His children, are going through—seeing how others have hurt, disappointed, and betrayed us. And instead of crying to Him and casting all our cares upon Him and receiving His loving embrace, we remain "on the bow," frozen in the sea of fear and in the entanglements of counterfeit affections, comforting ourselves with anger, control, and isolation. And all the time the Father is calling out to us: "Live! Live! Live!"

As I dropped Sarah off at school, I told her how much I just wanted to hold her while everyone else wanted to throw her away. "I'm not ashamed of you, Sarah—no matter whose fault this is. All that matters is that you're my little girl who I love. And I'm not ashamed to be your daddy. God is not ashamed of you (see Heb.

11:16), and Jesus is not ashamed to be called your brother" (see Heb. 2:11).

Later that day, Sarah came home and said, "Dad, I need to talk to you and Mom. I don't know what's the matter with me, but I need to talk. And Dad, I don't need a counselor! I need a father. I don't need any lectures, Dad. I need a hug."

As Trisha and I sat down with Sarah in my study, Sarah said, "Dad, I just don't know. When everything is going right in my life, all I want to do is hug you and be in your presence, but as soon as things aren't going my way, I just want to cut myself off from every other human being. It's like I would rather be alone on a deserted island somewhere and never see another human being again. I can't get hold of God's love. There seems to be a pattern in me where I can find God only when people are saying all the right things about me. But when they are not, I can't find Him, and I don't want to be with you."

As she was sharing her thoughts and feelings, I was thinking, *That's me!* When God is answering my prayers and doing everything I want Him to do, how quickly I run to Him! But when I feel like He's not doing what I want Him to do on my timetable, something in me shuts down and I find myself "on the bow" of the boat in the entanglements of the sea of fear.

I asked Sarah, "When did this begin? What comes to mind first when you think about closing your heart to love?"

She replied, "Dad, do you remember when you resigned as a Salvation Army officer and went back to captaining a fishing boat?"

"Yes."

"How old was I then?"

"You were five."

At that time I was captaining a businessman's sport-fishing yacht. It was like fishing out of a mansion, with a beautiful living room filled with overstuffed chairs and sofas.

"Do you remember the day Mom brought me down to the boat to see you?"

"Oh, yes, I remember."

Trisha had brought Sarah down to see me, and lowered her over the stern of the boat. When Sarah saw me sitting back in a comfortable chair in the living room of the yacht, my precious 5-year-old daughter came running to me for a hug. She leaped into my lap, knee first...and I suddenly got in touch with the deepest core pain of my life!

My response was an instinctive reaction of self-protection. I had no intention of wounding my daughter in any way, but as I started to fall to the floor in extreme agony, I threw Sarah 8 or 10 feet through the air onto the sofa on the other side of the room. Although I was rolling on the floor almost nauseous from the pain, my young daughter, while having suffered no physical injury, was experiencing a much deeper pain than I was. She had come running to enjoy her father's embrace only to be thrown away because she had failed to perform or act in the right way. She had risked opening up her heart to me...only to have it slammed shut.

How many times have you come and risked opening your heart for a moment of tenderness, a moment of nurturing, or a moment of warmth, only to receive nothing in return?

As Sarah was screaming and crying, I continued to hug and kiss her and did everything I could to make it up to her. After about ten minutes, she finally calmed down. Did I intentionally hurt my daughter? Of course not. But that was the moment Sarah had stopped opening her heart and receiving me as her father, and she had struggled with that feeling of rejection ever since. That night, as we prayed with Sarah, we didn't pray over the 17 year old; we prayed over the 5 year old. Something inside her burst loose in wailing, agonizing groans, and she wept and wept. For about 30 minutes, she lay cradled in my arms as we poured out love and comfort to her. It was a defining moment in Sarah's life—the beginning of realizing, "If my father, as broken a man as he, could comfort me at 17 years old, how much more does Father God want me to run to Him in every moment of crisis?"

We either live our life as if we have a home and a loving Father's arms to run to when the world is trying to give us what they think we deserve, or we live our life as if we don't have a home. We want to live in Dad's house and enjoy Dad's provisions, but like Sarah, who locked herself in the bedroom and came out only for what Dad could give her—food, credit cards, keys to the car—we fear an intimate relationship.

So, which will it be? Will you live your life like an orphan who has no home, frozen in numb-numb-ville on the bow in the midst of the sea of fear? Or will you live your life in the warmth of your Father's loving embrace, a perfect love that drives out all fear? (See 1 John 4:18.)

What would your life be like if you had no fear? The choice is yours: *Fear...or Father's Embrace?* I hope the remainder of this book helps you to choose *no fear!*

Endnote

1. Henri Nouwen, *The Return of the Prodigal Son* (New York, NY: Image Books, Doubleday, 1992).

CHAPTER TWO

AN ORPHAN HEART

Before we can live a life with no fear, we have to deal with the matter of an orphan heart. We all were born with an orphan heart that rejects parental authority and seeks to independently do everything our own way. The only humans who were not born with an orphan heart were Adam and Eve. Instead, they possessed a spirit of sonship from the very beginning but eventually exchanged it for an orphan heart when they chose to go their own way apart from God. As a result of their fall, their orphan heart passed down to every succeeding generation, thus becoming the common heritage of all humanity.

So, our quest is not to *regain* our sonship with the Father; we cannot regain something we never had. Rather, our quest is to enter into the embrace of the unconditional love of Father God and *receive* a heart of sonship that will *displace* our orphan heart. It took me many years to learn this truth. I was radically saved in 1980, radically filled with the Holy Spirit in 1984, and yet for many years afterward continued to live with an orphan heart. Growing up in a home environment of alcohol and emotional abuse with parents who, because of their own orphan hearts, did not know how to express love, I never learned how to be a son, and because I didn't know how to be a son, I didn't know how to be a good father either. Consequently, my family suffered for years.

When you possess an orphan heart, you never truly feel at home anywhere. You are afraid to trust, afraid of rejection, and afraid to open up your heart to receive love. And unless you are able to receive love, you cannot unconditionally express love, even to your own family. You can be born again, go to church every week, tithe, avidly study the Bible, and do all the right Christian "stuff," and still have an orphan heart. Being saved does not automatically mean feeling secure, loved, and accepted as a son or daughter of God; they are two different things. The new birth in Christ makes you a son or daughter of God, but that does not mean that you will enter automatically into the full personal experience of that love relationship with Him as Father.

This is why over and over and over again people come up to me at conferences I teach and confess, "I just can't get it. I've gone to dozens of conferences; I've heard the teachings on the Father's love; I've had countless hours of counseling and prayers for healing and deliverance; and I still cannot get free of fear and insecurity in my relationships." For a long time I did not know what to say to them because I suffered from the same problem—I still had an orphan heart.

A Stronghold of Oppression

Left unchecked, an orphan heart can grow into a stronghold of oppression—a habit structure of thinking or fortress of thought that is so deeply entrenched that only a profound experiential revelation of Father God's love can displace it.

My daughter, Sarah, was learning to trust my love until she was 5 years old. The orphan heart that she was born with was in the process of being displaced. As I said, you can't cast out an orphan heart. It is a heart that feels as if it has no home. It must be displaced, and the only way to do that is to introduce the orphan to a loving father. Then the orphan must choose to submit his or her heart to that love. Ideally, this should happen for all of us as children through the examples of a loving mother and father. But there are no perfect mothers and fathers. So what then? What happens if you run to a parent for love and comfort and affirmation, as Sarah did to me on that yacht when she was 5, only to feel hurt or rejected? Perceived rejection can be just as damaging to a child (or an adult) as intended rejection. Left unhealed or unresolved, the wound can set into motion in an orphan heart a 12-step progression that eventually manifests as a stronghold of oppression powerful enough to handicap a person for years emotionally and which prevents them from cultivating healthy loving and caring relationships.

1. *We begin to focus on the faults we see in parental authority.* I did not hurt Sarah intentionally; my response to her was an instinctive defensive mechanism. Her 5-year-old heart perceived it as rejection, however, and from that day on, I was no longer the wonderful daddy who could do no wrong in her eyes. She had opened her heart to me in childlike innocence but felt bruised and tossed aside. As a result, Sarah closed her heart to me that day. No matter what I did after that or how Sarah and I related to each other, a part of her heart was shut off to me because of the disappointment inside her, that she had once come to me with open arms and I had rejected her. Sarah's closed heart was her self-defense mechanism against being hurt again.

Our true personality is revealed in our family relationships. We can wear masks before the world, but home is where the masks come off. Even as children we notice the faults of our parents. We see how they misrepresent Father's love to us and recognize the disappointments, broken promises, and inconsistency in behavior. And these flaws can loom large in our eyes, leading to the next step.

2. *We receive parental faults as disappointment, discouragement, grief, or rejection.* Sarah interpreted my momentary instinctive defense response as my personal rejection of her. How often, whether with our children, our spouse, our work colleagues, or our fellow believers at church, do we throw someone aside as a reaction of our own personal defensive mechanism, leaving that person feeling wounded or rejected? We don't mean to do it, but it happens. None of us as parents intentionally hurt our children. We do not intentionally misrepresent the love of God. But we can give to others only what has been given to us. How can I ever be a father if I have never felt like a son?

As a child, although I had a father, I always felt more like a slave in his house than a son. There was no nurturing, tenderness, warmth, affection, comfort, or protection. And because I grew up feeling like a servant, that is how I treated my children. I could give to them only what had been given to me. Is it any surprise that they received it as woundedness and rejection? They didn't feel safe trusting me, which brings us to step number three.

3. *We lose basic trust in parental authority.* Once disappointed, rejected, or otherwise wounded by a parent, we close off a part of our heart to keep it from being hurt again. A wall goes up. A certain degree of basic trust is lost. Trust and basic trust are two different things. If I walk by you and accidentally step on your foot with my size 15 shoes and say, "Oh, I'm so sorry, please forgive me," you may still trust me as a person. But the next time I walk close by, you will make sure you withdraw your foot so it doesn't get tramped upon. You trust me as a person, but because of your past experience of pain inflicted by me, you fear that the same hurt may happen again. So you withdraw a part of yourself—the part that was injured before because a measure of your basic trust has been lost.

That's what happened with Sarah. She still trusted me as her father to love her, take care of her, and provide for her needs. She trusted me on surface relationships, "safe" conversations, and the like, but she no longer trusted me when it came to matters of intimacy and deep personal communication. Because I had hurt her deeply in that area, she did not trust me with her heart or her deep feelings.

When we discuss basic trust, we are not talking about the ability to believe or trust another person, but the capacity to hold your heart open to another person, especially if you believe his or her motives or intentions are questionable. Basic trust is the ability to risk being real and vulnerable, to keep your heart open even when it hurts rather than close off your spirit.

At its center, basic trust is an issue between you and God. Basic trust is when you are able to move beyond the weaknesses in others and receive God's healing touch, one moment at a time, and not run away; to retreat into His loving embrace and enter the place of sonship, even when someone close to you may be misrepresenting Father's love to you. It is taking on the Spirit of Christ, a meek and gentle heart, and entering into Father's rest, while casting all your cares upon Him. Loss of basic trust leads to the fourth step toward oppression.

4. *We move into a fear of receiving love, comfort, and admonition from others.* Once basic trust is lost, it becomes difficult to receive from others because we are afraid to make ourselves vulnerable. So when the inevitable crisis comes, our response is to just suck it up outwardly and take care of everything ourselves because we don't trust anyone else or believe there will be someone to comfort us. With an orphan heart, you often feel alone, especially in a crowd or during times of crisis.

5. *We develop a closed spirit.* Once we close our hearts to receiving love, we close our hearts to intimacy (in-to-me-see). We retreat into a closed spirit, isolating our heart from outside influence and

from all but the most superficial or unhealthy emotional attachments. Intimacy is lost.

6. *We take on an independent, self-reliant attitude.* A closed and isolated heart manifests itself with an attitude that says, "If anything is going to get done around here, I'll have to do it myself." Our insecurities and fears have shut our heart off from any meaningful relationships with others. Independence and self-reliance are often cherished and valued qualities in our culture. While they may seem to be important and useful in the political or business arenas, they are deadly in relationships, family, and community and can result in restlessness and disease because we are not able to cast all our cares upon Him. Instead, we carry them all ourselves, which leads to the next step.

7. *We start controlling our relationships.* With an orphan heart, our independence and isolation are nothing more than issues of control. They may manifest as agitation or apathy. We limit our relationships and conversation to "safe" topics like news, sports, weather, etc. The fear of trusting, fear of rejection, and fear of intimacy prevent us from tackling deeper subjects and from allowing anyone to become more personal with us.

8. *Our relationships become superficial.* With a closed heart, healthy relationships are very difficult. The three fears listed above unconsciously influence us to keep others at arm's length emotionally. And we rarely realize that we are doing to them the very same thing we fear they will do to us: rejection.

9. *We develop an ungodly belief that says no one will be there to meet our need.* That is the danger of an independent, self-reliant heart. Not only are we afraid to depend on someone else, but we also feel that no one values us enough to care for us.

I closed my heart to receiving my mother's and father's love when I was 12 years old. As a result, I took on an independent, defiant, controlling, and rebellious attitude that hurt me as much as it hurt them. There was no sense of sonship (honor, respect, and interdependence), which leads to number ten.

10. *We begin to live life like a spiritual orphan*. An orphan heart feels that it does not have a safe and secure place in a father's heart where they feel loved, valued, and affirmed. We have no safe harbor, no refuge, no place of rest. Outside of our identity being in what we do, we really have nowhere to call home. We believe that we will have to argue, wrangle, and fight for anything we want to accomplish in life. With no place to call home, we start seeking love in all the wrong places.

11. *We begin chasing after counterfeit affections*. Having shut ourselves off from the genuine affections of family and friends, we start looking for counterfeit affections—substitutes for the affections we left behind at home or never had. We were created for love and family; consequently, without them, we will find something to bond to as a replacement, even if it is unhealthy or destructive.

I classify counterfeit affections under the "seven P's": passion, possession, position, performance, people, place, and power. *Passions* of the flesh often take the form of various addictions: food, alcohol, drugs, sex, pornography, escapism—whatever seems to comfort our lonely and insecure heart. Some people turn to *possessions*, thinking that they somehow will find their heart's rest through worldly gain. Still others seek *position*—the praise of man, seeking acceptance by striving to be seen or by slaving away in an effort to win the approval of others, especially of those who can advance our lot in life. *Performance* feels that there is something more you must do or put in order before you can find rest and feel good about yourself. *People* is a belief that a person or spouse is the answer to all your needs instead of making God's love your primary source. *Place* is an ungodly belief that, "If only I had a better job, I would be happy...if only I lived somewhere else...if only I could run away and escape...." Finally, *power*-seekers desire to control their own life and destiny, with little desire to be open or real and with little sense of need for anything from anybody. Control of emotions, people, or circumstance is their way of making sure they are never disappointed or hurt again. This, of course, is totally unrealistic. Counterfeit affections bring no true fulfillment and easily lead to the 12th and final step.

12. *We begin to daily battle a stronghold of oppression.* Having isolated ourselves from cultivating healthy relationships, we become trapped in a cycle of seeking fulfillment in things that can never satisfy. Unable to receive love, acceptance, and admonition either from God or from others, life for us becomes an oppressive mix of tension, agitation, anger, bitterness, restlessness, and frustration that can eventually lead to depression.

Restoring the Father's Heart

A life of oppression, spawned by an orphan heart, is the common experience of almost every person. Even among Christians, who know the truth of forgiveness of sins and eternal life through faith in Christ, only a small percentage have truly experienced the full embrace of Father's love. Their troubled marriages, families, and relationships are evidence of this fact. Too many Christians are still caught up in the entanglements of the orphan heart. Consequently, few have learned to displace their orphan heart with a heart of sonship.

That number is growing, however. An orphan heart is common in a fallen, sin-ridden, competitive world, but it was never God's desire or plan for us. And He is actively at work to change the situation. In our own generation, we are witnessing the beginnings of the restoration of Father's heart to the hearts of His children, just as foretold in Scripture. The Book of Malachi, the final Book of the Old Testament, closes with a wonderful and powerful promise:

> *See, I will send you the prophet Elijah before that great and dreadful day of the Lord comes. He will turn the hearts of the fathers to the children, and the hearts of the children to their fathers; or else I will come and strike the land with a curse* (Malachi 4:5-6).

The promise of God is that *"the prophet Elijah"* will come *"before that great and dreadful day"* when Christ comes. We know from Jesus' own words in the Gospels that this promise was fulfilled once in the person of John the Baptist, who came to prepare the way for the coming of the Lord. However, this prophecy also contains a deeper dimension of meaning that relates to the end of the age. Before Christ returns, Elijah will come, this time in the form of an anointing or movement rather than embodied in one person. Why "Elijah"? It was Elijah who was instrumental in overthrowing abusive and controlling authority when he defeated Jezebel's prophets. Later, when Elijah was taken up to Heaven in a chariot of fire, Elisha, his spiritual son who witnessed his ascension, called out, *"My father, my father..."* (2 Kings 2:12). Then in Malachi, "Elijah" represents a fathering anointing that will be released on the earth in the endtimes. Malachi 4:6 bears this out in its description of the effect the release of this anointing will have on the world—to *"turn the hearts of the fathers to their children, and the hearts of the children to their fathers."* Thus, the curse of the orphan heart will be displaced.

Until and unless Elijah comes, the land remains under a curse. And what is that curse? *A feeling of fatherlessness.* More than at any other time in human history, fatherlessness is the curse of our generation. Today more children than ever before are growing up in fatherless households, and many more are growing up without a father emotionally, even though their biological father is physically present in the home.

One of my own greatest personal challenges in life today is being a father. As I said before, how could I be a father if I had never felt like a son? My mom and dad were always emotionally detached and distant, and many of you, I am sure, could share similar stories. It has been only within the last ten years, after I received the revelation of Father's love and of sonship, that my parents and I have begun to make the emotional connection we had been missing for many years.

Millions of children today are growing up feeling as though they don't have a home. When I say "home," I'm speaking of a place of warmth, protection, comfort, security, and identity—a place where we receive a sense of purpose and destiny and a reason to get out of bed in the morning. Home is the place we can run to when things go wrong, the place where we can receive affirmation and encouragement, not so much for what we have done but for whose son or daughter we are. Home is the place where we belong and cease striving and enter into rest.

Unfortunately, for many of us, this is not the home life of our experience or memory. One study has revealed that, for most Christians, 80 percent of our thinking is negative and in agreement with the enemy, the accuser of the brethren, who tells us we have no value or are unlovable, and who feeds our orphan heart ungodly beliefs about God's loving nature so that we live as if we don't have a home even though we are children of the King.

An orphan spirit can reside over an individual person, over a church, over a city, over a region, or even over a nation. And wherever an orphan heart holds sway, whether individually or corporately, people get up every day feeling like they don't belong. They do not feel accepted. They have little sense of being valued, honored, or loved. Their lives are defined by their perceived need to perform in order to be approved and affirmed.

Those who are secure in Father's heart, on the other hand, know they are loved and accepted for who they are as God's creation, not for what they do. They know they don't have to perform; they don't have to strive hard to meet up to all the rigid demands of what a "good Christian" ought to be. They know that they are loved *just the way they are.*

In these endtimes, before a major spiritual reformation hits the earth, there will first be a deeper revelation of the heart of the Father that breaks the orphan spirit on the earth today. This is not an automatic product of salvation. Unless our orphan heart is displaced by the revelation of Father's love, even as Christians we can end up battling oppression every day of our lives. Such was the experience of the late Derrick Prince.

Eighty Years Finding Home

Derrick Prince was arguably one of the greatest Christian leaders and evangelists of the 20th century. His evangelistic crusades routinely drew tens of thousands of people to each meeting. Across more than 50 years of ministry, he saw millions of people saved, filled with the Holy Spirit, healed of diseases, and delivered of demonic oppression. Few Christian leaders of the last century established ministries as credible and anointed of the Lord as his. Yet, by his own admission, Derrick Prince himself battled demonic oppression every day of his life until he was 80 years old. Millions were set free under his ministry, yet he himself could not find freedom from the oppression that dogged him on a daily basis. It took nothing less than a powerful personal experiential revelation of Father God's love to set him free once and for all. Here is the story in his own words, as appeared in his February 1998 newsletter:

> My understanding of God was revolutionized by a personal experience in 1996. Ruth and I had been sitting up in bed one morning praying together as we normally do, and I became aware of a powerful force at work in my feet

and lower legs, and it moved upward until my whole body was forcibly shaken by it. Ruth told me later that the skin on my face changed to a deep red, but at the same time I was aware of an arm stretched out towards my head, seeking to press down something like a black skull cap upon me.

For a few moments there was a conflict between these two forces, then the power at work in my body prevailed, and the arm with the skull cap was forcibly taken away and vanished. Immediately, without any mental process of reasoning, I knew that I could now call God my Father. I had used the phrase "our Father" for more than 50 years. Doctrinally I was clear about this truth; I'd even preached a series of three messages on knowing God as Father, but what I received at that moment was a direct personal revelation.

Let me share with you my interpretation of this experience. I was born in India, and spent the first five years of my life there. Twenty years later, after I was saved and baptized in the Holy Spirit, I became aware of some dark shadow from India that always hung over me. I understood it was one of India's gods that had followed me through life, seeking to oppress me. There was one particular way that this god oppressed me. Every morning I would awake with a dark foreboding of something evil awaiting me. It was never anything precise, just some amorphous darkness. This unknown evil never actually happened, but every day the foreboding was there.

After I was baptized in the Holy Spirit the foreboding diminished in intensity, but it never disappeared. I did, however, discover that if I set my mind to praise and worship, the foreboding would lift from me, yet it always came back the next morning.

Can you identify with Derrick's experience? How many times have you gotten up in the morning feeling like you don't have a home, that there is so little expressed love, little comfort, conditional acceptance, and a diminishing hope for experiencing lasting peace and rest? You feel a sense of oppression, a sense of foreboding, a sense of impending disaster. Most mornings you face another day of pain, another day of fear, another day of people saying all the wrong things about you, another day of not measuring up in the eyes of the people who matter to you the most, another day of wondering whether or not you will survive.

How do you go on living like that? How do you go on, knowing that tomorrow you have to get up and do battle with all of it again? Is not the cross of Christ more powerful than the darkness we have to fight our way through every day? This has nothing to do with salvation but everything to do with experiencing and understanding Father God's love.

Continuing his story, Derrick says:

> The day that black skull cap was pulled away the foreboding vanished, never to return, and from that morning it became completely natural for me to now address God as Father, or my Father. I now have a personal relationship, not just a theological position. I've been enjoying this new relationship for about two years.
>
> Ever since I was saved I have believed that if I continued faithful to the Lord, I will go to heaven when I die, but I never really thought of heaven as my home. After that arm with the black skull cap was taken away, however, it has now become natural to view heaven as my home. Shortly afterwards I said to Ruth, "When I die, if you want to give me a tombstone you can just write on it two words: Gone Home."

Derrick's experience illustrates the truth that it is one thing to know God as Father, but another thing to *experience* Him as Father in a deeply personal way. Although Derrick Prince was born again, filled with the Holy Spirit, and powerfully anointed and effective in ministry for over 50 years, until he was 80 he still had an orphan heart and battled oppression every day.

John the apostle, in the first of his three letters, clearly separates knowing from believing: "*We have come to know and have believed the love which God has for us...*" (1 John 4:16a NAS). It is easy to believe in our minds that God loves us, but like Derrick Prince we can live our entire lives never *knowing* that love in our hearts in a deeply personal experiential way.

Don't Wait 'Til You "Go Home" to Go Home

Even as Christians we can live—and die—with an orphan heart. Many, unfortunately, do just that. It almost happened to Derrick Prince. Had it not been for his profound experience in Father's love in 1996 when he was 80 years old, he might well have finished his days on earth without ever truly feeling like a son in his Father's house.

You don't have to wait 'til you "go home" to experience a home-coming; you can enter that place of rest, refuge, and safety right now. Jesus said, "*I came that they may have life, and have it abundant-ly*" (John 10:10b NAS). Abundant life means a fulfilled, satisfying life here on earth as well as eternal life in Heaven, and a fulfilled life means displacing the orphan heart with a heart of sonship.

Jesus Christ came from the Father and after His resurrection, returned to the Father so that we too may abide in Father's embrace. John, in fact, says that He "*is in the bosom of the Father*" (John 1:18b NAS). That phrase speaks of deep intimacy, unity, and oneness. And where Jesus is, He wants us to be also:

In My Father's house are many rooms; if it were not so, I would have told you. I am going there to prepare a place for you. And if I go and prepare a place for you, I will come back and take you to be with Me that you also may be where I am (John 14:2-3).

We all can experience this intimacy, oneness, and sense of sonship with the Father in this life because of the presence of the Holy Spirit in our lives. Jesus is saying, "There's a place for you in Dad's house. That's where I am, and I'm getting your place ready. I will not leave you as an orphan but will come to you, and Father and I will make Our home in you" (see John 14:18-23).

God is love. And feeling secure as sons and daughters in His fatherly embrace is what everything in creation is all about. The Kingdom of Heaven is all about love, joy, and peace, and being free from fear, insecurity, and anxiety. Perfect love is what characterizes Heaven, and God's perfect unconditional fatherly love is available to you each day—no fear, anxiety, anger, bitterness, hurt feelings, or resentment.

There's a place for you in Father's heart right now, where you can live your life hearing His voice saying to you every day, "You are the child I love and in whom I am well pleased." The center of all creation is being at home in Father's heart. His heart is a place of rest from our striving, but few have entered into that place of rest. Why?

It doesn't necessarily depend on your home environment where you grow up—whether your home was a good home or a bad home, or how loving your parents were. You could have been raised in a very good, loving Christian home environment, yet have spent your entire life like Derrick Prince, battling oppression every day. Just because you were brought up in a good home does not automatically mean you will not struggle with an orphan heart—living your life as though you don't have a home versus living it as if you do. It's not a matter of whether you came from a home filled with nurturing, tenderness, and gentleness, or a home in which no love was ever expressed.

More importantly, it's a matter of displacing your orphan heart and embracing sonship; and until you do, you may find it difficult to abide in Father's embrace. Before this can happen, however, one of the first things you must do is decide *whose mission you are on—God's mission, your own mission, or somebody else's mission.*

CHAPTER THREE

WHOSE MISSION
ARE YOU ON?

During my years as a commercial snapper fishing boat captain, I generally fished with a four-man crew. Needless to say, those four men living in close quarters together at sea on a 44-foot boat for seven days often resulted in some very interesting relational dynamics. During one trip, I hired on as a deck hand one of the top captains in the fleet who was presently without a boat. I soon learned that two emotionally immature captains working the same fishing boat go together like oil and water.

Steve thought that he knew more than me—what rock pile to fish on next, when to move the boat, what bait to use, and so on. You could say he did not take kindly to me as captain nor to my fishing style. Like most captains (me included) he was submitted to no man and to no mission but his own. It was a week of agitation, arguments, competition, and one fistfight. In fact, so much energy was given to our rivalry that we battled fatigue all week, which diminished our harvest of fish. Lesson learned— you can have only one captain on a boat, and no matter how good you think are, if you are going to reap a successful harvest, the crew had better be willing to be subject to the captain's mission, or you will end up wasting time trying to work out each other's differences.

Whether we are aware of it or not, each of us is on a mission that determines our future harvest in life and relationships. For some of us, our life mission is more clearly defined than it is for others. And the source of our life mission—its point of origin— will determine whether we live life feeling like a spiritual orphan or as if we are a spiritual son or daughter. So, the basic question each of us has to answer is: *Whose mission am I on?*

We have one of two choices. We will be subject either to the Father of Creation's mission or to the mission of the father of lies, the accuser of the brethren. These are the only possibilities. Even if we think we are subject to our *own* mission, we are really serving the mission of our enemy, because anything that diverts us from following Father's mission weakens our life and relationships and advances satan's purposes on earth.

Be Subject to Father's Mission

Our problem is that too often we don't see ourselves as Father's favored sons and daughters; rather, we feel more like spiritual orphans. The writer of Hebrews states it like this:

> *It is for discipline that you endure; God deals with you as with sons; for what son is there whom his father does not discipline? But if you are without discipline, of which all have become partakers, then you are illegitimate children and not sons* (Hebrews 12:7-8 NAS).

God deals with us as *sons*, which in this context should be considered a generic word that includes *daughters* as well. The focus of these verses is not gender, but *relationship*. God relates to us not on casual terms as servants or even as friends, but intimately as beloved children. All of creation is about Father God longing for a personal intimate relationship with us as His sons and daughters.

One inevitable part of this Father/child relationship is discipline. Father God's discipline is, in fact, evidence that we are His sons and daughters. Absence of discipline means absence of relationship. This is why the writer says, *"But if you are without discipline...then you are illegitimate children and not sons."*

How are you about receiving discipline? What do you do when someone close to you—your spouse, your prayer partner, a leader of your small group, or your boss, for example—takes you aside and says, "You know, I've been watching the way you relate to others and have observed a pattern in your life that really concerns me. Can we talk about it?" Doesn't it give you warm fuzzies to know that someone cares enough about you to risk confronting you? Doesn't it make you want to say, "Oh, yes, tell me more!"? Or does it rub your fur the wrong way?

If someone is trying to bring truth or admonition to your life and you resist it, then you are like an illegitimate child and not a son or daughter, at least in heart attitude. Inability to receive discipline can be a sign of an orphan heart. Orphan hearts have an independent spirit and resist admonition and correction. Whereas, sons and daughters welcome these things, even when they seem unpleasant. They know these parts of discipline are a crucial part of the process of nurture and growth to maturity. More importantly, they embrace discipline as proof that they are favored children of a caring Father.

Recently, some of my closest friends and board members at Shiloh Place Ministries sat down with me and said, "Jack, there is a relational pattern in your life that really concerns us."

Reluctantly, and a little apprehensively, I replied, "I probably need to hear more." This was significant because for nearly 50 years I *didn't* want to hear it. My orphan mind-set was not open to constructive criticism and correction. After I received the sonship revelation, however, I began welcoming corrective admonition because I knew it would help me learn to think and act like a son.

The "concern" my friends and colleagues shared with me was a heavy one, and my first thought was defensive, *Wait a minute! You do the same thing! And you're teaming up two-to-one on me?* But then I remembered this Scripture from Hebrews that says if I cannot receive discipline—if I struggle against receiving admonition and correction in my life—then I am like an illegitimate child and not a son.

The Greek word for *illegitimate* literally means, "bastard." When we refuse to receive discipline, admonition, or correction, we isolate a part of our heart from other people, including God. In effect, we become fatherless. We either live our life as if we have a home, or we live our life as if we don't have a home. We live life valuing admonition, or we reject it and take on an orphan heart.

Kinder than the word *bastard* is the phrase "spiritual orphan." A spiritual orphan is a person who feels that he or she does not have a home or a safe and secure place in a father's heart where he or she feels loved, accepted, protected, affirmed, nurtured, and disciplined.

Hebrews 12:9 brings us to the issue of our mission: *"Furthermore, we had earthly fathers to discipline us, and we respected them; shall we not much rather be subject to the Father of spirits, and live?"* (NAS). When we are subject to the "Father of spirits," life flows. The Greek word for *subject* literally means "dependent" and "underneath." Furthermore, the words subject, *subjection*, and *submission* are all interchangeable in Greek. I like to paraphrase the last part of this verse to say, "Be subject to Father's mission and live." Be in submission to, get underneath, and be dependent upon

Father's mission…and life begins to flow in our emotions and relationships.

But what is the opposite? Be subject to your own mission—self-protection, independence, self-reliance, not opening your heart to love or to the possibility of being hurt again—and death comes. Paul's words in Romans bear this out:

> *For the mind set on the flesh is death, but the mind set on the Spirit is life and peace, because the mind set on the flesh is hostile toward God; for it does not subject itself to the law of God, for it is not even able to do so, and those who are in the flesh cannot please God* (Romans 8:6-8 NAS).

To be subject to our own mission is to be led by our flesh, which leads to death, but to be subject to our Father's mission leads to life and peace. Is your life and relationships at peace? Or is death slowly at work all around you? Your answer to those questions may determine what your life and your relationships—as well as those of your children and grandchildren—may be like in the future. Be subject to your own mission, and barrenness will work its way into your emotions and relationships. Be subject to the Father's mission, and life and peace will begin to flow through you—spirit, soul, and body.

What Is Father's Mission?

If pursuing our own mission leads to the lack of lasting fruitfulness, while the Father's mission leads to life and peace, then it is important to know what Father's mission is. Simply stated, Father's mission is *for you to experience His expressed love and to give it away to the next person you meet.* Successful execution of Father's mission is a matter of combining two elements in the proper order and balance—the scriptural mandates many Christians know as the "Great Commandment" and the "Great Commission."

Many believers consider the Great Commission the lifeblood of evangelical Christianity. This is, of course, Jesus' well-known charge to His followers just before He ascended to Heaven 40 days after His resurrection:

> Go and make disciples of all nations, baptizing them in the name of the Father and of the Son and of the Holy Spirit, and teaching them to obey everything I have commanded you. And surely I am with you always, to the very end of the age (Matthew 28:19-20).

Who could deny that winning souls is seen as a top priority in the Kingdom of God? After all, the Bible says that Jesus came to earth and died on the Cross so that all people could be reconciled to God and that those who are reconciled have been charged with the ministry of reconciling others (see 2 Cor. 5:18-19). When I was in Bible school, the Great Commission was the emphasis that rose above all others. It was stressed even to the point of implying that unless you were willing to forsake your family and everybody else in order to "go," then the sincerity of your commitment was in question.

As important as the Great Commission is, it is frequently overemphasized to the point of neglecting, and sometimes forgetting, another mission that is even more important—the Great Commandment. One day a religious leader asked Jesus what was the greatest and most important commandment in the law.

> Jesus replied: "'Love the Lord your God with all your heart and with all your soul and with all your mind.' This is the first and greatest commandment. And the second is like it: 'Love your neighbor as yourself.' All the Law and the Prophets hang on these two commandments" (Matthew 22:37-40).

In effect, Jesus was saying, "When you seek to know God's love and to make it known, you are released from every other obligation in the Word of God." Romans 13:8-10 tells us that love is the fulfillment of the law. Love is to be the inspiration, the driving force behind everything the Church does, including fulfilling the Great Commission. Jesus left no doubt about the priority of love:

A new command I give you: Love one another. As I have loved you, so you must love one another. By this all men will know that you are My disciples, if you love one another (John 13:34-35).

John stressed the same point:

Dear friends, let us love one another, for love comes from God. Everyone who loves has been born of God and knows God. …This is love: not that we loved God, but that He loved us and sent His Son as an atoning sacrifice for our sins. Dear friends, since God so loved us, we also ought to love one another (1 John 4:7,10-11).

Paul went so far as to say that without love, nothing else we do matters:

If I speak in the tongues of men and of angels, but have not love, I am only a resounding gong or a clanging cymbal. If I have the gift of prophecy and can fathom all mysteries and all knowledge, and if I have a faith that can move mountains, but have not love, I am nothing. If I give all I possess to the poor and surrender my body to the flames, but have not love, I gain noth-ing (1 Corinthians 13:1-3).

It is in this Great Commandment to love God and to love oth-ers where we find the Father's mission. His desire for us is that we receive His love and give it away, thus fulfilling the Great Commission.

The Great Commandment to love God and love others is a call to intimacy; the Great Commission to go and make disciples is a call to fruitfulness. Intimacy is to precede fruitfulness. The Great Commandment must precede the Great Commission and is an inseparable part of it. When intimacy does not precede fruitfulness, we easily become subject to our own mission and become focused upon religious duty, hyper-religious activity, and aggressive striving that leaves an angry edge in our life and relationships.

How do you recognize a person who truly knows and loves God? By how well he or she can preach? By how many people fall down in the Spirit when they pray? Because they have faith to move mountains? By how they relate to others at church on Sunday? By how much Bible they know? No. You recognize a person who knows God by the life of love, compassion, and tenderness he or she shows behind closed doors with family and peers when no one else is looking. A person who loves God is one who seeks for the love of God to be made mature and complete in his or her daily relationships. I love the way The Message Bible paraphrases it: *"God is love. When we take up permanent residence in a life of love, we live in God and God lives in us. This way, love has the run of the house, becomes at home and mature in us..."* (1 John 4:17-18, TM).

What is the key for the world to come to know God's love? *Agape*, a love that seeks the low place of humility, service, honor, and value. And that's where we find God's mission. The Great Commandment is to be fulfilled before the Great Commission. But those with orphan thinking are easily deceived, as I was for many years, into placing the Great Commission ahead of the Great Commandment. They become more committed to justice, duty, or ministry than to intimacy. Intimacy must precede fruitfulness. When it does not, we usually end up becoming subject to our own mission, often leaving behind us a trail of fractured relationships where we have misrepresented the love of God to our families, peers, and to the world.

Any time you put the Great Commission (your ministry) before the Great Commandment (your relationship), you step outside being subject to Father's mission, and death starts working its way into your relationships. I'm not necessarily talking about physical death, but the great "numb-numb-ville" on the bow on the sea of fear (see Chapter One), frozen with no ability to move or to free yourself from the entanglements that come when you're subject to your own mission. You trade the security of home and sonship for the fear and uncertainty of homelessness and an orphan heart.

Exposing the Root of the Orphan Heart

Every one of us has to deal at some point with the manifestations of an orphan heart. It doesn't matter whether you were raised in a dysfunctional home or a stable, well-established home. Even growing up in a good home filled with a father's unconditional love and acceptance does not necessarily mean that you will not struggle with orphan thinking and be subject to your own mission.

Consider the examples of the prodigal son and his older brother in Luke 15. Although they were surrounded by the deep compassionate love of their father, each of them had an orphan heart that prevented him from enjoying intimacy with his father. The older son was angry and saw his father as someone to obey, while the younger son saw his father as someone who could give him things. Neither son related to his father on an intimate level. It took the younger son leaving home and becoming destitute before he came to his senses, returned to his father, and embraced the sonship that had always been his. As for the older son, Scripture gives no indication that he ever reached that point.

Because we all were born with an orphan heart, we all are subject to our own mission from birth. Think about it—is a 2 year old subject to his father's mission or to his own mission? What about a 12 year old or an 18 year old? Our orphan heart problem stems all the way back to the Garden of Eden, where our first human parents were deceived by lucifer, the original spiritual orphan.

Lucifer did not start out as an orphan, however. He began in beauty and splendor, surrounded by the glory and love of Father God:

> You were in Eden, the garden of God; every precious stone adorned you: ruby, topaz and emerald, chrysolite, onyx and jasper, sapphire, turquoise and beryl. Your settings and mountings were made of gold; on the day you were created they were prepared. You were anointed as a guardian cherub, for so I ordained you. You were on the holy mount of God; you walked among the fiery stones. You were blameless in your ways from the day you were created till wickedness was found in you (Ezekiel 28:13-15).

Not only was lucifer continually in the presence of God, he was also the worship leader in Heaven. But that was not enough; he wanted more. And in his greedy attempts to get more, lucifer lost everything. Isaiah vividly describes the disaster:

> How you have fallen from heaven, O morning star, son of the dawn! You have been cast down to the earth, you who once laid low the nations! You said in your heart, "I will ascend to heaven; I will raise my throne above the stars of God; I will sit enthroned on the mount of assembly, on the utmost heights of the sacred mountain. I will ascend above the tops of the clouds; I will make myself like the Most High." But you are brought down to the grave, to the depths of the pit (Isaiah 14:12-15).

This powerful prophetic image of lucifer, or satan, also reveals his "job description": to lay low or weaken the nations. How does he do it? By using the orphan heart to get us into orphan thinking.

God is love. The Kingdom of Heaven is all about perfect love, joy, and peace with no fear, insecurity, or anxiety. Lucifer dwelt there in the beginning and reveled continually in God's perfect love. At some point, however, something in lucifer desired to be subject no longer to God's mission but to be dedicated to his own mission. Anytime we become subject to our own mission, separation goes to work. Lucifer subsequently lost the privilege of dwelling in the Father's house of unconditional love and acceptance. He was separated from his Creator and from his home. As Isaiah says, *"Your iniquities have separated you from your God; your sins have hidden His face from you, so that He will not hear"* (Isa. 59:2).

Lucifer became the ultimate spiritual orphan. Separated from his original home, he became resentful toward anyone who enjoyed intimacy with Father God, particularly those human beings God had created in His own image. Because he no longer walked in Father's mission of love, lucifer began to compete for a place of recognition, position, and power.

Jealousy drove lucifer to deceive Adam and Eve. The tool he used to cripple mankind and weaken the nations was orphan thinking. His strategy was to convince man to think the way he did—homeless and cut off from God's love—and thereby weaken man to the point where he would give in to temptation and allow shame and fear to replace intimacy.

Satan's thoughts were, *I will do it my way. I will pursue the things that make me feel good and give me a sense of value and significance!* And because Adam and Eve bought into his orphan thinking, they, as well as we, have received his orphan heart as part of the "package deal."

Trouble in Paradise

Having failed in his bid to rule Heaven, lucifer lost his right to have a home in Heaven. He then immediately set his sights on Adam and Eve, who lived in innocence, joy, and in open, loving fellowship with the Father. That's the way it often is with spiritual orphans—they do everything possible to make sure that everyone around them is just as unhappy as they are.

In the meantime, Adam and Eve were at home in the Garden of Eden, every fiber of their beings warmed by the unconditional expressed love of Father God. They fellowshipped with their Father face-to-face, continually tasting and drinking deeply of His affectionate love. They walked openly and innocently before Him and with each other with no fear, shame, or embarrassment. No clouds of doubt or uncertainty dimmed the light of their peace and joy.

Meanwhile, satan looked on this scene with bitterness and hatred, envious of the love and intimacy with God they enjoyed and which had once been his as well. People with an orphan heart are envious of anyone who enjoys true love and intimacy. Lucifer was determined to destroy it.

The quickest way to shut down intimacy and trust is by sowing seeds of doubt into the relationship. Appearing in the form of a serpent, lucifer approached Eve and led her to question God's character and integrity.

> "Did God really say, 'You must not eat from any tree in the garden'?" The woman said to the serpent, "We may eat fruit from the trees in the garden, but God did say, 'You must not eat fruit from the tree that is in the middle of the garden, and you must not touch it, or you will die.'" "You will not surely die," the serpent said to the woman. "For God knows that when you eat of it your eyes will be opened, and you will be like God, knowing good and

evil." When the woman saw that the fruit of the tree was good for food and pleasing to the eye, and also desirable for gaining wisdom, she took some and ate it. She also gave some to her husband, who was with her, and he ate it. Then the eyes of both of them were opened, and they realized they were naked; so they sewed fig leaves together and made coverings for themselves (Genesis 3:1b-7).

Adam and Eve desired to be like their Father, forgetting perhaps that, because they were made in God's image, they were already like Him. But satan insinuated that God was holding out on them. He tried to steal from them their understanding of how God thought of them. That's where orphan thinking begins—you start doubting Father's love, kindness, and generosity towards you. From there, it is only a short step to doubting the love of others around you, including family.

Doubt about God's love for them led Adam and Eve to doubt His mission. In their desire to become "like God," they chose to abandon Father's mission and pursue their own mission. In other words, they tried to become like God through orphan thinking—which never works. It is impossible to be free as long as your thoughts and attitudes are in agreement with the father of lies.

Taking the Shortcut

Eve was deceived, while Adam sinned deliberately. Paul makes this distinction when he writes: "*And it was not Adam who was deceived, but the woman being deceived, fell into transgression*" (1 Tim. 2:14 NAS); and "*…sin entered the world through one man, and death through sin, and in this way death came to all men, because all sinned…death reigned from the time of Adam to the time of Moses, even over those who did not sin by breaking a command, as did Adam…*"

(Rom. 5:12,14). So Adam, then, actually entered into sin willingly, while Eve was deceived by orphan thinking.

The Father's command was, "Don't eat the fruit from the tree in the middle of the garden." Adam and Eve's desire was, "If we do this our way, we'll more quickly mature and become like God, and He'll appreciate and value us more."

Do you see how orphan thinking confuses the issue? It may sound perfectly logical and reasonable on the surface, but it never leads where we think it will. Instead of leading us closer to God, orphan thinking leads us away from Him—and prevents us from drawing close. I call orphan thinking the "shortcut spirit" because we think that *our* way will take us where we want to go more quickly than being subject to Father's mission. Adam and Eve wanted to please God; they wanted a place in His heart, and thought that through their human effort they could get there more quickly. However, seeking to do it their way led them far away from Him instead.

There was now no turning back for Adam and Eve. Having disobeyed God, they no longer had the sense of sweet fellowship and kinship they had before. They were now thinking and acting like orphans without a home, which is why they hid when they heard the sound of God walking in the Garden. Look how quickly relationships deteriorate under an orphan spirit. No sooner had God confronted Adam about his sin than Adam turned on his wife:

> "Have you eaten from the tree that I commanded you not to eat from?" The man said, "The woman You put here with me—she gave me some fruit from the tree, and I ate it" (Genesis 3:11b-12).

Instead of protecting his wife from orphan thinking, Adam blamed her; and trust and intimacy between them were lost. Even today, because the orphan heart is so strong, genuine trust and intimacy are two of the most difficult qualities to develop and maintain in a relationship.

The loss of trust and intimacy then opened the door for guilt and shame to rush in. However, because God loved Adam and Eve so much, He would not allow them to go uncovered and live in shame. He shed the blood of an animal and used its skin to clothe them. This is a perfect illustration showing that no matter how far outside Father's house we live, Father still wants to cover us. As Peter wrote, *"Love each other deeply, because love covers over a multitude of sins"* (1 Pet. 4:8).

God is not ashamed to be called our God (see Heb. 11:16), and Jesus is not ashamed to call us brothers (see Heb. 2:11). As Christians covered by Jesus' sacrifice, God does not judge us, condemn us, or accuse us (see John 3:16-18; 5:22-24; 12:47-48). He loves us and wants to cover us. Yet Adam blamed Eve for his sin and for their trouble, and she refused to take ownership of her deception, opting instead to pass the buck to the one who deceived her. Thus, Adam and Eve by default chose orphan thinking over being restored into Father's love.

Consequently, Father God was left with no choice but to displace them from living life in a home. How it must have broken His fatherly heart when He had to drive Adam and Eve from the Garden. But they could not stay as long as they were under the sway of orphan thinking. Their orphan thinking had separated them from the Father, and so they had to leave. God drove them out for another reason as well—mercy. As long as Adam and Eve remained in the Garden, they were in danger of eating fruit from the tree of life and living forever in their alienated, orphan-heart state (see Gen. 3:22-23).

Adam and Eve's sin and ensuing departure from Eden (home) were the source of all subsequent despair on the earth among men. Fear, anxiety, torment—they all began at this point. Mankind lost all sense of living as if he had a home. Every human born in every subsequent generation was now born with an orphan heart and became subject to his own mission; then death, which always involves separation, entered in. The death at work in an orphan heart is separation from God, separation from any sense of having a home, and separation from friends and family because of broken trust.

All of this homelessness, despair, broken trust, separation, and alienation are why these words of Jesus are central to the Gospel: "*I will not leave you as orphans; I will come to you*" (John 14:18). We have a home anytime we want it, whenever we are ready to give up the life of orphan thinking and return to the warm embrace of our Father's love.

Spirits in Conflict

Today, as in all the ages of human history, two spirits are in constant conflict on earth for our hearts. The first of these is the spirit of *sonship*, which we can also call the spirit of Isaac, Abraham's heir and the son of promise. People possessed of this spirit live life as if they have a home. Their destiny is sure and secure.

On the other hand, in conflict with the spirit of sonship is the *orphan* spirit, which causes people to live life as if they don't have a home. We can call this the spirit of Ishmael, who was Abraham's natural son by Hagar, his wife Sarah's handmaid, but who was not included in the inheritance promised to Isaac. While Isaac grew up blessed and lived in anticipation of his inheritance, Ishmael and his mother were sent away. It was said of Ishmael, "*He will be a wild donkey of a man; his hand will be against everyone and everyone's hand against him, and he will live in hostility toward all his brothers*" (Gen. 16:12). History bears this out. Ishmael's descendants (the Arab nations) settled near Egypt, far from the land of Canaan, and have lived in almost continual conflict with Isaac's descendants, the nation of Israel.

This describes the orphan spirit—independent; hostile; contentious; with no sense of home, belonging, or of being a son. Quite often, the natural foreshadows the spiritual. In other words, earthly events frequently reflect heavenly realities, revealing what is happening in the spiritual realm (see 1 Cor. 15:46).

Today, in the Arab-Israeli conflict, the orphan heart continues to fight for control and domination of those who possess the spirit of sonship. Although the Arabs, who are descendants of Ishmael, own 50 times as much land as do the Jews, who are Isaac's descendants, they continue to fight to take away what little Israel has.

In the nations of the earth, the orphan heart is waging all-out war against sonship. Lucifer's orphan thinking has weakened the nations in their understanding of God as a loving, compassionate, and affectionate father. This war is also within the Church, within the business realm, within our families, and within the hearts and minds of individuals. The orphan spirit has gained control of the world system as humankind has become subject to his own mission rather than to the mission of Father God.

The orphan spirit is a heart attitude and a mental stronghold that is a temptation for all of us. But it can also become a demonic stronghold over a person, a church, a workplace, a city, or even a nation.

If you (or a church) have an orphan spirit, as I did for a long time, you feel as though you don't belong. Love, value, honor, and acceptance are foreign concepts to you. You believe you have to act right, dress right, talk right, and do right in order to be loved and accepted; and even then, it still doesn't happen. You feel as if there is something more you have to do or put in order to find rest and feel valued. With a spirit of sonship, however, you feel loved, valued, honored, and accepted for who you are as God's creation. You have no need to "prove" yourself to anyone. As a son or daughter, you feel a sense of total love and acceptance. Contrarily, as an orphan, you feel like you are on the outside looking in, trying as hard as you can to perform and be good enough to earn a place in someone's heart.

When wanting to cast out an orphan heart, remember that you can displace it only by introducing it to a loving Father. Even then, an orphan heart must choose to embrace the spirit of sonship by willingly becoming interdependent in relationships and embracing God's community of love. This is not a once-and-for-all choice. You choose sonship over and over because orphan thinking doesn't surrender easily, and it often comes back and tries to assert its influence once again. The orphan spirit tries constantly to weaken our families, relationships, and the nations by deceiving us into becoming subject to our own mission rather than living life to experience God's love and to give it away.

Choose Father's Mission

Home is always there for us. By "home," I mean the place where we find rest from our striving in God's unconditional love and acceptance. In Christ, we are forgiven and loved, and yet we can still choose our own way. Remember that intimacy precedes fruitfulness. We can't have a fully meaningful, purposeful, and productive life and healthy relationships until we embrace a heart of sonship with our Father—until we choose to be subject to His mission and find in Him the warm, deep intimacy we have always hungered for. It is in being subject to Father's mission that we find His strength and life flowing through us and humbling us so that love and intimacy become the motivating factors of our life and ministry.

It was this kind of loving and intimate relationship with God that Paul had in mind when he prayed:

> ...*that Christ may dwell in your hearts through faith. And I pray that you, being rooted and established in love, may have power, together with all the saints, to grasp how wide and long and high and deep is the love of Christ, and to know this love that surpasses knowledge—that you may be filled to the measure of all the fullness of God* (Ephesians 3:17-19).

When we begin to displace our orphan spirit by receiving and embracing the spirit of sonship, putting the Great Commandment ahead of the Great Commission will become perfectly natural. Much of what passes today for Great Commission ministry and evangelism has been influenced by orphan thinking, resulting in placing the Great Commission ahead of the Great Commandment. The brokenness of so many families of Christian leaders evidence that fact. Our tendency is to live by the love of law instead of by the law of love. Is it any wonder, then, that the church of today, despite having greater resources available than ever before in history, has not turned the world upside down the way the apostles and other early Christians did in the Book of Acts?

If we are more concerned with ministry than with the needs of our family, then whose mission are we subject to? Satan's plan is to weaken the nations, and he does this by weakening families first. If satan cannot stop us from doing good things, he will keep us so busy doing good things for others that we neglect our own children who end up feeling like they don't have a place in our heart, and they too become spiritual orphans.

It's time to displace this cycle. It's time to unfasten the lifeline and abandon the wind-tossed, sleet-whipped bow on the sea of fear for the warmth and safety of the wheelhouse. It's time to stop and wake up from the "numb-numb-ville" of being subject to the enemy's death-dealing mission and take up the mantle of life as beloved sons and daughters whose hearts are focused upon Father's mission.

To Be Like Jesus

In the eighth chapter of Romans, Paul talks about this idea of sonship:

> ...those who are led by the Spirit of God are sons of God. For you did not receive a spirit that makes you a slave again to fear, but you received the Spirit of sonship. And by Him we cry, "Abba, Father." The Spirit Himself testifies with our spirit that we are God's children. Now if we are children, then we are heirs—heirs of God and co-heirs with Christ (Romans 8:14-17a).

Here we find the very heart of sonship. But in order to come into this place of sonship, we have to be led by the Spirit of God, who is a fathering Spirit. He is not a Spirit of slavery leading us into a life of fear again, but the Spirit of sonship. This Spirit of sonship is a Spirit of intimacy and innocence. *Abba* is a Hebrew term of endearment that essentially means the same as "Daddy." It is a term of intimacy, spoken by children who are in the presence of a loving Father whom they love and trust. In Daddy's presence there is no fear, no bondage, no oppression, and no anxiety.

The Holy Spirit gives us the inner assurance that we are children of God. And because we are children of God, we are also heirs of God and co-heirs with Christ. To be led by the Spirit of God means to be subject to Father's mission, and our perfect example for this is the life of Jesus, our Elder Brother. How did Jesus view His mission? He had only one mission—the mission given Him by His Father: "*I tell you the truth, the Son can do nothing by Himself; He can do only what He sees His Father doing, because whatever the*

Father does the Son also does" (John 5:19). And Jesus was completely faithful to Father's mission. The night before He was crucified, He prayed: *"I have brought You glory on earth by completing the work You gave Me to do"* (John 17:4).

Everything we see in Christ we are heirs to as Christians. The goal of our Christian life is to become like Jesus. But we don't become like Jesus by focusing our lives on Jesus; we become like Jesus by focusing our lives on what Jesus focused His life on. And Jesus focused His life on being a Son and revealing the Father and His love so that a world of spiritual orphans could become sons and daughters. Jesus wasn't sinless because He was God; it wasn't His divinity that made Him the man He was. Jesus was the man He was because of the Father He had. The person each of us becomes will be determined by who we focus our life on.

A little later in His prayer, Jesus prayed for all His followers:

> *I have given them the glory that You gave Me, that they may be one as We are one: I in them and You in Me. May they be brought to complete unity to let the world know that You sent Me and have loved them even as You have loved Me* (John 17:22-23).

The whole mission of creation is about receiving love and bringing us into unity. That is why Jesus commanded us to love each other as a testimony to the world (see John 13:34-35). Father's mission is that the entire world experience His love by the love that flows in and through us as we receive His love and give it to the next person we meet. That is our mission in life. It is what we were created for. Every fiber of our being was created to receive love and give it away. Nothing in life is more natural than walking in the love of our Father and passing that unconditional love on to others. On the contrary, the orphan spirit is unnatural, and causes us to be unnatural as long as we allow it to influence us.

We will be subject to one of these two missions—the Father's mission or satan's mission—depending on the choices we make. So, choose Father's mission. Follow Jesus' example and focus your life upon being a son, finding life and peace. Be a gift of love to the next person you meet.

CHAPTER FOUR

NO SONSHIP,
NO INHERITANCE

For a seaman looking to escape an impending storm, nothing is more comforting than reaching safe harbor.

In Antarctica, safe harbor for a sailing vessel can be hard to find because almost everywhere you go along the Antarctic Peninsula you encounter nothing but sheer mountainous cliffs, icebergs, and glaciers calving at the water's edge. In addition to the ice, weather conditions can change without warning, in an instant turning the most beautiful scenery on earth into the most treacherous and life threatening. A sudden drop in temperature or change in wind direction can turn a safe anchorage into a deadly trap as encroaching pack ice and bergs threaten to crush the hull of any small boat unlucky enough to get caught there.

One secure anchorage that has a small sheltered cove is Port Charcot. Named for a French explorer, Port Charcot was a welcome safe harbor during our eight-man sailing expedition to Antarctica where we pulled in shortly before a snowstorm hit. All around us the ice floes froze up causing us to spend two days there among the penguin colonies.

Finally, when the ice began to clear as shifting winds pushed it away from the coastline, the captain told us that we had a 14- to 16-hour window of good weather to motor another 30 miles farther south to a Ukrainian research station, where we could spend a day or two. Here we were in a safe harbor at Port Charcot, knowing a severe storm was on the horizon, yet something drew us out. We were willing to risk leaving our refuge for "greener pastures," so to speak, to sail into unknown waters on our quest for adventure.

So, in the morning, we set out under engine power, and for a couple of hours made pretty good progress. Our 74-foot aluminum sailboat crunched steadily through the seams in the pack ice that was up to one-foot thick. Yet as we continued, the ice kept our speed down to two or three knots, and a few miles from safe harbor at the Ukrainian research station, the pack ice began to thicken to the point that we could see no water in the bay. Eventually, we found ourselves completely surrounded by ice. We couldn't back up because putting the engine in reverse would have sucked ice into the propeller and destroyed it. Our extraordinary and exhilarating journey now threatened to become a fight for our lives.

The captain assured us that we were perfectly safe as long as there was no wind. Under calm conditions, we could handle the pack ice. If the wind kicked up, however, the pressure from the pack ice mixed with icebergs could move in and crush our vessel. Here we were, 600 miles from the nearest civilization, with ice closing in all around us, so we had to climb 50 feet up into the rigging of the mast and try to spot small seams and breaks in the pack ice where we could force our way through. With each minute that passed, the captain's tone became a little more urgent, reinforcing our need to reach the Ukrainian research station before the approaching blizzard hit around 10 o'clock that night.

So Near, and Yet So Far

Finally, at about 6 o'clock, when we had only a mile to go to reach the research station, we discovered that we were unable to make any more headway. We knew that safe harbor lay just ahead, but because the ice had grown so thick, the captain said we would have to turn around and go back before the wind picked up!

Go back? But we were so close—indeed, almost close enough to see the station on the other side of the island! Just half a mile ahead of us, another sailing vessel was making the turn to starboard that would bring it around to the lee side of the small island where the research station was located—the side that would be ice free. With our own eyes, we could see the other vessel moving into safe harbor, yet we could not get there ourselves!

Because we couldn't back up, we used little seams in the pack ice to turn around. It was a disheartening and agonizingly slow process, but gradually we managed to reverse direction and began motoring north again through the pack ice, slowly pushing aside small bergs that were sitting five and ten feet deep off either side.

At 10 o'clock at night, still daylight because the sun never sets during the Antarctic summer, the wind grew stronger and stronger, eventually reaching a velocity of 50 knots on the wind gauge. Ice, sleet, and snow were blowing sideways, and visibility dropped to under 100 yards. Although we had finally broken out of the pack ice, we were now surrounded by giant icebergs fighting simply to find our way home into safe harbor once more.

We were in the middle of a gale trying to run north in an effort to reach safety, with only two places within 40 miles where we could even consider tying up our boat. Finally, we pulled once more into the cove at Port Charcot. We could not simply drop anchor, however, because the wind and the ice could shift without warning causing the vessel to swing wildly and possibly run aground. Instead, we had to tie down by launching a 12-foot rubber Zodiac raft and then run four lines to the shoreline from the bow and stern, both port and starboard—all in the middle of a freezing blizzard.

About the time we got the boat tied down, the wind shifted and icebergs anywhere from 10- to 20-feet high began moving into the little cove, threatening to crush our vessel. One iceberg finally lodged against our hull, and we had to use the motorized Zodiac to drag our vessel out of harm's way because, once again, we could not use reverse gear because of the ice. In one moment's turn of circumstances, what had looked like safe harbor became a deadly trap that threatened to destroy us. But the harbor had looked so secure—so welcome! And besides, earlier we had camped out there for two days, and it *was* safe then. But it all depended on which way the wind was blowing and how that wind would cause the pack ice to pile up in that cove.

We fought for two hours to get out of that ice trap, finally making it back out into an open bay. Icebergs were everywhere, the gale was blowing at 50 knots plus, and we wondered where we were going to go now in the midst of this blizzard. The captain said our only choice was to head for Port Lockroy 20 miles to the north—if we could make it without running into any icebergs. Our boat was equipped with radar, but the blizzard with its wildly blowing snow seriously degraded its accuracy. Each man confronted his fears as we battled through 20 miles of raging winds and sleet blowing sideways. Every few minutes someone had to run up onto the forward deck and throw a bucket of water on the windshield because we could hardly see through the Plexiglas frozen into a slab of ice.

I could never describe to you the joy and liberation we felt, after fighting our way from morning until after midnight through pack ice, gale-force winds and blizzard, passing within feet of icebergs, and working our way up through the narrow Neumayer Channel, to finally enter Port Lockroy, surely one of the most beautiful places on earth! Upon rounding a bend at the head of the channel, suddenly the sun broke out and all around us, 360°, were mountains up to 5,000 feet high, covered with snow and glaciers in each valley! Inside Port Lockroy's little bay, it was as calm as it could be because the mountains were blocking most of the winds. Outside was the fury and danger of the storm while inside all was peace and calm in a little haven of safety that for over 100 years had saved the lives of many whalers and other mariners.

Our Quest for Safe Harbor

A safe haven from the storms of life is what each one of us is searching for, but still so many can't seem to find their way home. We either search for a safe harbor we have never known or seek to return to the safe harbor that once was ours, but have lost our way. At one time, we knew safe harbor. We tasted of Christ's forgiveness, salvation, and peace. But through the circumstances of life, the sins of others against us, or our sins against others, we have found ourselves battling a blizzard, in the middle of a whiteout. With our vision blurred, it becomes difficult to hear the comforting and affirming voice of God. We struggle with the consequences of decisions we made, thinking we were pursuing something "better" in life, only to have fallen into a well-laid trap of the enemy that threatens to ice us in and freeze us into numb-numb-ville.

There is safe harbor, ready and waiting for us. We are on a quest for home again. God's love is reaching out to us to guide us into that place of safety and security. But that safe harbor is reserved for sons and daughters, not those with an orphan heart. A life of peace, rest, and fruitfulness in Father's embrace is our inheritance, but only those who are dedicated to Father's mission find it. Orphans subject to their own mission remain outside safe harbor, buffeted and blown by the wind and the waves, and limited in vision and hopefulness.

In Antarctica, even with all my years at sea as a licensed fishing boat captain, I did not know the way to safe anchorages or how to overcome such violent storms. Therefore, I chose to trust the captain of the expedition who had been there so many times before. I surrendered my independence and my pride as an experienced sea captain and became a "son" subject to another captain and to his mission, which was to lead all eight of us to a place of comfort and warmth.

Our quest for safe harbor begins when we acknowledge our need to give up the independence and self-reliance of the orphan heart and humble ourselves willingly to be fathered and mothered by other men and women who have been there before, people who know how to find their way through the storms and the gales of life and who know where safe harbor lies. Safe harbor—the heart and love of the Father, along with all the riches and resources of His Kingdom—is our inheritance when we enter in with a heart of sons and daughters. Whose son are you? Whose daughter are you? Remember—no sonship, no inheritance.

In the previous chapter, we looked briefly at what Paul had to say about sonship in Romans 8. Let's examine that passage here in a little more detail.

> For all who are being led by the Spirit of God, these are sons of God. For you have not received a spirit of slavery leading to fear again, but you have received a spirit of adoption as sons by which we cry out, "Abba! Father!" The Spirit Himself testifies with our spirit that we are children of God, and if children, heirs

*also, heirs of God and fellow heirs with Christ if indeed we suf-
fer with Him so that we may also be glorified with Him. For I
consider that the sufferings of this present time are not worthy
to be compared with the glory that is to be revealed to us*
(Romans 8:14-18 NAS).

*"For all who are being led by the Spirit of God, these are sons of
God."* In verse 5, Paul says that either we walk in and are led by the
flesh, or we walk in and are led by the Spirit. Walking by the flesh
leads to death while walking by the Spirit leads to life and peace.
If we are led by the Spirit, we are subject to Father's mission and
life will flow. There will be growth and fruitfulness. A sense of
unity and a sense of the fruit of the Spirit will begin to grow in us.
We will begin to mature in our emotions and relationships. If, on
the other hand, we are subject to our own mission, death will flow,
and we will find ourselves becoming more independent and isolated in our relationships.

Movement toward the Father's mission and away from living in
darkness comes by focusing our life upon what Jesus focused His
life upon. We don't become like Jesus by focusing our life upon
Jesus; we become like Jesus by focusing our life upon what Jesus
focused His life upon. Jesus said, *"When you pray, say, 'Our
Father....'"* Over and over again—150 times in the Gospel of John
alone—Jesus makes reference to focusing our life upon the Father.
And there is no the way to the Father but through the Son.

How do you begin movement toward a homecoming in Father's
embrace? By focusing your life on being a son or daughter. But if
you are subject to your own mission, there is little spiritual growth.
You find yourself in numb-numb-ville, surrounded by pack ice,
with an inability to move forward in your Christian walk. You
might see around you others making movement through the ice,
but you remain frozen; you become locked in a sea of excuses,
blame-shifting, and justifying. Your insecurity with love and relationships has stagnated your growth and maturity.

So look how movement begins in verse 14: *"For all who are being led by the Spirit of God"*—all who are subject to Father's mission—*"these are sons of God"* (NAS) This word "sons," means "mature sons." Another word used for "child of God" is *teknon*, which refers to an immature child who lives for what others can do for him or her. Who is it that is going to move forward into the Kingdom of God? Those who have a spirit of sonship or a spirit of adoption. Verse 15 says, *"For you have not received a spirit of slavery leading to fear again, but you have received a spirit of adoption as sons by which we cry out, 'Abba! Father!'"* This spirit of sonship or spirit of adoption is not the Holy Spirit but a heart attitude of being at rest in Father's embrace. It is like saying, "That person has a meek or gentle spirit." We either have a spirit of sonship or an orphan spirit; there is no middle ground. And whatever spirit we have determines whether or not we will enter into our inheritance— experiencing Kingdom life on earth.

Let me try to make this revelation alive with everyday life and language.

A Frustrated Dream

My whole childhood dream was to be a fishing boat captain. Growing up in Daytona Beach, Florida, a few blocks from the beach, I didn't want to play tennis the way my father wanted me to; I wanted to captain a fishing boat. I fished every day of the year from the Main Street pier or the Main Street bridge. The house I grew up in, and where my mother lived for 53 years, was one block from Boot Hill Saloon, four blocks from the ocean, and three blocks from the oyster beds in the intracoastal waterway. I lived every day fishing, catching trout, snook, bass, drum, whiting, and flounder. My whole dream was to become the best fishing boat captain there was.

But the interesting thing about the fishing business is that it is one of the most difficult professions in the world to get into. Anyone can fish, but being a professional is usually passed down from father to son or father to daughter. Certain businesses and trades are kept secret and passed down as a generational inheritance from mom and dad to the next generation and the next generation and the next. If a fishing boat captain teaches his mate or any other member of his crew all his secrets, that person might become a captain of his own boat and steal his former employer's fishing spots. It is a highly secret, competitive, every-man-for-himself business. Few boat captains will teach anyone anything except his children. It is the children's inheritance.

When I was 13, I began working as the mate on a boat at Ponce Inlet that belonged to one of my dad's best friends. He had three sons and captained a six-passenger sport fishing boat, fishing for mackerel, tuna, mahi-mahi, and billfish. Often his sons were on the boat. And it was the most aggravating thing for me as a mate to be on that boat with the father and his sons. I wanted so much to say, "Captain, please take me up in the wheelhouse. Teach me how to run a boat. Teach me how to find fish. Teach me navigation." I said nothing, and he left me on the deck to cut bait. The sons rarely did anything! They just sat up there with their father while he taught them everything about being a captain. Later, two of them became some of the best.

I was supposed to be on the boat an hour each time before it sailed, and I was always there early because I was determined to have the cleanest and most well-organized boat. I worked harder than anybody else because I had to prove to the captain that I had value. "Teach me, train me, help me grow in the profession! That's my dream!" But I wasn't a son. Those who were the sons would come in with their father at the last minute, and he would pour his life into them. It seemed to me that I did all the work and the sons got all the benefits!

This is where many Christians live. They see a select few upon whom God seems to pour out His greatest blessings. "Look what God has done in Jack's life! He just pours out and blesses him. Jack must be one of His favorites. God will do it for others, but He will never do it for me." That's an orphan attitude.

My dead-end situation working as a mate on boats made me agitated and angry until one day I finally said, "I've had it!" and quit. I felt that nobody was ever going to teach me anything, so I gave up on my dream. I lost myself for awhile in the whole hippie and drug culture in Daytona Beach. After a few scrapes with the law, and after growing tired of people using me and then throwing me away when I was no longer useful to them, I decided to go back to fishing and paid a visit to a family friend in the fishing business.

"Captain Johnny," I asked, "do you know of anybody who needs a good mate?"

"Yes, I do," he replied. "Captain Kline. He has three vessels now—a brand-new 70-footer, a 55-footer, and a 45-footer. No one wants to work the 25-year-old 45-footer. He can't keep a mate on her. Start there. As hard as you work, you won't have any trouble working your way up."

So I went to see Captain Kline, who hired me and put me to work as the mate on that old 45-foot boat, the *Snow White I*. While everybody else wanted to work on the other boats because they were newer and finer, I set out to prove myself to the Captain. I really slaved away on that boat and poured my life into it; and any day we weren't at sea, I was there eight or ten hours trying to work my way to the top.

As a slave or servant, you feel you must work harder to succeed. You have to strive, outperform, and outdo everybody else just to prove that you have a right to be. But sons and daughters? On their day off, they're usually not working hard trying to prove a point. They don't have to come in early or stay late. Why should they? They already own the boat anyway because Dad will one day turn everything over to them. They just sit in the wheelhouse and learn all the easy and fun parts of fishing—piloting the boat, navigation, finding the fish. Those with an orphan heart are left to do the dirty work.

Many Christians feel like a hired hand with no inheritance. An orphan has no expectation of comfort, provision, or promotion because he knows that the son will receive the inheritance. And so, even if the orphan works harder and harder, trying to earn his way, he usually winds up angry or apathetic.

Look again at the passage in Romans 8: *"For you have not received a spirit of slavery leading to fear again, but you have received a spirit of adoption as sons by which we cry out, 'Abba! Father!' The Spirit Himself testifies with our spirit that we are children of God"* (Rom. 8:15-16 NAS). Inheritance is for mature sons and daughters. Who will give a $1 million inheritance to a 10 year old and let him loose? There is no inheritance for children until they grow up and are willing to take responsibility for their parents' mission.

A Dream Come True

Captain Kline had spent over 40 years at sea, including service on PT boats during World War II. After the war, he had moved to Ponce Inlet, Florida and gone into the fishing business, owning and operating the *Snow White* fleet, which eventually included three vessels. And before long, he had earned a reputation as one of the most respected and prosperous fishing boat captains in the industry.

Now, after 40 years at sea, Captain Kline wanted to get out of the business, but there was a problem—he had no son or someone he could trust to whom he could pass on his business, his legacy, and his name. Captain Kline and his wife had always dreamed of having children, but it had never come to pass; and considering other people in the professional fishing community was really not an option, because generally they have more than their share of dysfunctional characters and alcoholics. Many are unsettled and routinely jump from boat to boat every few months. Drinking and brawling are commonplace, and when I first went to work for Captain Kline, my background was not much different...except for one matter—I was driven to succeed, to do everything I could to prove that I deserved a place at the top.

Although I was the newest and lowest of eight mates on the three boats in the fleet, I always arrived earlier than any of the others and usually stayed later. My determination paid off quickly. Within a couple of months after I began working on the *Snow White I*, Captain Kline said to me, "This old boat looks better than it has in ten years!" He continued watching me and sometime later said, "Jack, you appear to be one of the best mates I have ever seen. I've never had a man as conscientious as you." I always kept the cleanest and most well-organized boat and was always the first to arrive and the last to leave. When Captain Kline fired his first mate on the new 70-foot boat, the *Snow White III*, he promoted me to that position ahead of all the others. The other mates—spiritual orphans like me—were mad, of course, because they all wanted that spot. Orphans are always looking for the high place, the place where they are recognized and affirmed. And because they have no inheritance, they feel the need to scrape, scramble, and fight for everything they want.

Then one day Captain Kline said to me, "Jack, you know I have no son to take over the business, and after 40 years at sea, I've had enough. Stick with me, Jack, and I'll teach you everything I know. I'll train you to be a captain and when you're ready, I'll turn the whole business over to you. Just hang with me and all this will be yours."

I could hardly believe what he was telling me. My dream was coming true! I was going to be a fishing boat captain! All I had to do was stay close to Captain Kline for a couple of years until I learned everything he could teach me, and then he would turn everything over to me. I would be the son he had never had and this would be my inheritance.

"Don't worry, Captain Kline," I said. "I'll stick with you." He then began to teach me everything about the boat. In the mornings, he would take me into the engine room and teach me how to listen to every sound those engines made, how to notice every flaw, how to determine if a seal needed to be replaced, simply by listening for a certain drip in a particular area of the engine. He would teach me how to know when a part was about to break down. In fact, I came to know those two big, turbo-charged V12 Detroit engines so well that I could have maintained them in my sleep. And within six months, Captain Kline no longer felt the need to personally go down in the engine room. He would simply come aboard and ask me, "Did you check the engines out?" because he *trusted* me. This was part of my inheritance.

Captain Kline even took me into the wheelhouse where only *sons* entered in! He taught me how to operate the boat, how to pilot and steer. He taught me navigation. He taught me how to use the fish finder, not only how to locate fish but also how to identify fish by the shapes of their schools. "This is a school of amberjack; this is a school of bait fish; this is what red snapper looks like; this is grouper; here is a school of king mackerel. Here is a rock ledge; notice where the fish are hanging. You're going to have to anchor the boat and allow for the wind and current; you don't want to drop the lines until the boat is sitting right on this little spot." Within a year, I was running his boat. The only thing Captain Kline had to do was sit back in his bunk while I—his *son*—took the boat out to sea to find the fish. And at the end of the day, I took it back in.

This was Captain Kline's legacy...and my inheritance. For two years, I made myself completely available to Captain Kline. Anything he needed, I was right there. It was easy; anybody could have had a spirit of sonship with someone as tender and gentle as Captain Kline was as a father to me.

Don't get me wrong; Captain Kline was a hard, tough man. He had a drinking problem stemming from his service in the war, where he witnessed much combat, blood, and death. A transfer five days earlier is the only thing that kept him from being killed with the rest of his PT boat crew when a direct hit destroyed the vessel. Like most others in the fishing industry, Captain Kline spent a lot of time in the waterfront bars. He was quite a scrapper and never one to back down from a fight. In fact, he often instigated them. When I began training under him, he often took me into the bars with him where he would seek out the biggest, toughest-looking guy in the place, tap him on the shoulder, and say, "My name is Al Kline, I'm 5 foot 9, and I can whip your ____ anytime." Then he would push me in front of him! I learned real quickly how to think and talk on my feet!

Learning Pains

Yet despite his tough demeanor, Captain Kline was always gentle and kind toward me. I was the son he had never had. Never once did he ever demean, criticize, or tear me down.

I remember the first time he told me to dock the boat. "Jack," he said, "you've got to pull it up, spin it around 180 degrees, line it up between those two pilings, and give it reverse throttle before you drift out of alignment."

Operating a boat at sea is one thing; docking it into a narrow slip against a three-knot current with the wind blowing is another. Add to that the close proximity of dozens of other boats and an audience of 60 tourists on deck, and you can understand how terrified I was. "I can't do it, Captain Kline. I can't do it!" I was scared to death.

Captain Kline walked over, put his hand on my shoulder, looked me straight in the eye, and said, "Don't worry, Jack. I'm right here behind you. You can do this. I believe in you, Jack."

When a father believes in you, you'll try anything. I did exactly what he told me to do. I pulled in, turned 180 degrees, lined up with the slip, threw the throttles into reverse...and took out the pilings. I hadn't been quick enough and had drifted out of position before reversing the throttle. As soon as it happened I ducked, expecting the barrage of abusive words and rage over my failure, such as I would have gotten at home. But they never came. Captain Kline just stood there with his hand on my shoulder and said softly, "That's okay, Jack. I'll take care of the pilings. Pull it out and let's try it again."

"I can't do it, Captain Kline. I can't do it." I was almost in tears. On the deck below some of the tourists were cursing and screaming, "What's the matter with that idiot kid up there in the wheelhouse?"

"You can do it, Jack," Captain Kline assured me. "In 40 years at sea I've never seen anyone as conscientious as you. I've never seen anyone who learns as quickly as you do. You can do this. You're going to be the best. Pull it on out. I believe in you."

So I pulled the boat out. Captain Kline refused to touch the wheel or the throttle. I moved upstream a little ways and then came back around. I lined the boat up just as before and gave it reverse throttle. This time the boat backed neatly into the slip. I risked failure but succeeded because I had a "father" who believed in me. And I started believing in myself. From that day through the 2,000 days of captaining fishing boats that followed, I never had another docking accident. That doesn't mean I never made any more mistakes. Captain Kline was one of the greatest men I have ever known and I would have done anything for him—anything to please him.

One day, when we had no charters, Captain Kline was two decks below in the engine room changing the fuel filters while I was in the wheelhouse polishing the brass when I decided to push the throttle levers forward out of their neutral position into wide open so that I could polish the chrome on and around the throttles more easily. That was all fine and good except that when I finished polishing the controls, I forgot to return the throttles to neutral.

Having finished in the wheelhouse, I joined Captain Kline below deck in the engine room where he had finished replacing the fuel filters and was ready to crank the engines to test for leaks. There was a start button near the engines and Captain Kline pressed it. Unlike modern cars, which will not start with the transmission in gear, boat engines do not have such a safeguard. As soon as Captain Kline pressed that start button, that turbocharged V12 engine roared to life *wide open!* The boat jumped forward, popping dock lines left and right, and started to take out part of the dock. Captain Kline screamed, "Who put the boat in gear? Who put the boat in gear?"

I shot out of the engine room and up two decks to the wheelhouse. By then, only one dock line was still holding, and if it broke, the boat would take out a dozen or so private yachts beyond. Frantically, I jerked the throttles down into neutral, and as the boat settled down, Captain Kline burst into the wheelhouse right behind me, still screaming, "Who put the boat in gear? Who put the boat in gear?"

At that moment, if my orphan heart could have blamed anybody else, I would have, but he and I were the only ones on board. The boat was drifting out, held by one dock line, the dock had sustained severe damage, and I had almost destroyed many thousands of dollars worth of yachts. I hung my head in shame and humiliation at my failure. Then, in my greatest moment of failure and embarrassment, Captain Kline started laughing, a deep belly laugh.

I looked up in amazement. With a big smile on his face, Captain Kline said, "I bet you'll never do *that* again!"

He didn't yell at me! He didn't ridicule me! He didn't condemn me! Instead, he showed me that it was okay to fail every now and then in the process of learning. He also assured me that he would pay for repairing the dock. Even in my moment of greatest failure, Captain Kline gave me the gift of honor. That's what a father does.

The Test of Sonship

Captain Kline loved me like a son, and I loved him like a father. But that was not enough because I still had an orphan heart. Although I didn't realize it at the time, my relationship with Captain Kline was built around what he was doing *for me*—he was fulfilling my dream to be a fishing boat captain.

For two years, he poured into me his 40 years of knowledge and experience with the sea and with captaining fishing boats. He promised me, "Jack, once you have your 730 days at sea, pass the Coast Guard exam, and get your Captain's license, I'll make you the captain of the boat. Then later, we'll draw up a contract, and you'll be owner of the fleet one day. I'll live off the payments, and the fleet will be yours."

Who wouldn't be faithful and loyal with that type of deal? For two years I never failed to do anything Captain Kline told me to do. I obeyed every command and followed every instruction. I was like a son, and he was like a father to me. But you can't measure sonship—you can't measure true loyalty and faithfulness—simply by outward obedience, because outward obedience can still mask an orphan heart.

In the story of the prodigal son in Luke 15, the angry older brother never left home, never demanded his inheritance early, and never disobeyed his father; but as the story reveals, he was obedient for all the wrong reasons. He never connected with his father's heart, and he felt like a slave and an orphan even in his father's house.

Unconsciously, my relationship with Captain Kline was based upon what he could do for me and not for relationship. Outwardly, it looked as though I was subject to Captain Kline's mission, but in reality I was subject to my own mission. Captain Kline wanted to raise up a son to whom he could leave a legacy. My orphan heart was more interested in fulfillment of my dream. We never really know what spirit is in us until our father, boss, or pastor makes a decision that does not benefit us—and then our true heart is revealed. We do not know what we are full of until we have been bumped—and then our true selves spill over.

One day, believing that the time was right for me to be captain, I approached Captain Kline. His response was not what I expected. "I'm sorry, Jack," he said. "I know what I promised you, but I can't do it yet. My wife has cancer, and her care and treatment are draining every dollar we have. I can't afford it right now. Stay with me through this crisis, Jack, and all this will be yours, just as I promised."

Those words were not exactly what I wanted to hear. I thought I was ready to captain a fishing boat. Captain Kline had promised it to me, and now I felt that he was breaking his promise. At that moment, I closed my spirit to him and went right down that 12-step progression from an orphan heart to a spirit of oppression that we discussed in Chapter Two. My orphan heart influenced me to make choices that were subject to the mission of the father of lies. I regarded Captain Kline's response as personal rejection and offense. He had promised to make me captain but had not followed through. While technically true, that reality was also colored by my orphan's attitude of what was "right' and "fair" to me. There was no room in my heart for decisions or actions that were right and fair for Captain Kline.

As my heart closed to him, I bought into other lies: "He doesn't care about you. All he wanted was your service. He's just been stringing you along." Captain Kline *did* want my service; that much was true. But he had always intended to reward my service with an inheritance. From the perspective of my closed heart, however, I could no longer see it that way. This man who had poured his life and his heart into me for two years; this man who had paid me twice as much as most other mates because he loved me and wanted to make sure I was taken care of; this man who put me on a year-round salary instead of seasonal pay; this man who was my best friend and the first man I had ever really let into my life—and the only thing I could think about was that he had deceived me. I felt he was cheating me out of what was rightfully mine.

Captain Kline tried reasoning with me numerous times, but my orphan heart was so closed to him that I couldn't receive what he was trying to say. I still worked the boat every day, but I refused to go up in the wheelhouse. He assured me that the captaincy was still mine someday if I would just hang in there with him for a little while longer, but I wouldn't hear it. You see, orphans rarely look to the future. Their vision extends no farther than what makes them feel right immediately and comforts their pain *now*. I felt like I had been denied what was mine, and that was that. And in my mind, my feelings of being "right" justified my negative attitude. Subsequently, my heart was prepared to be deceived by an "angel of light."

Inheritance Forsaken

The accuser of the brethren often comes to us as an angel of light in our moment of crisis. Usually, this angel of light is in the form of another person or opportunity that appears to promise blessing and fulfillment in our life. In my case, it was another boat owner whose captain wasn't making him much money working his boat. He knew that Captain Kline had poured all his knowledge and experience into me, including knowledge of the locations of all his top fishing spots. Each captain possesses his own list of painstakingly acquired fishing spots that he keeps secret from everyone else because they provide him with a competitive edge. Any mate who has acquired (stolen) a fishing location from his captain can walk into any waterfront bar and sell it on the spot for as much as a thousand dollars. That's how important they are.

This boat owner came up to me and said, "I see Captain Kline hasn't made you captain yet. You know, it may be years before he does…if ever. I think he's just taking advantage of you. I tell you what—if you come to work as captain for me, you'll probably double your salary the first year."

Even after considering these tempting words, I was still reluctant to leave Captain Kline after all he had done for me, so I tried to persuade him to follow through on his promise. I was tired of waiting. But he still had to say, "I'm sorry, Jack, but I can't do it right now. Please bear with me. Hang on a little longer, and you'll be captain soon."

When I realized that Captain Kline was not going to budge, I said, "In that case, I give you my two weeks' notice."

To this day, I can still see his face, tears welling up in the eyes of this man who had stopped crying in battle while on the PT boats during the war 35 years earlier. I remember how he set his shoulders and went into the fighting stance that he had adopted in the bars when he was getting ready to pick a fight. Struggling to hold back the tears, Captain Kline said, "No, Jack. Either stay with me or get off my boat right now."

"What will you do without a first mate? You've got 60 people coming on board today. None of your other mates even know what they're doing."

"I'd rather have them than you. Get off my boat." His heart was breaking.

So I walked off his boat and over to the other boat owner. "I accept your offer," and he made me captain that very same day. I didn't think about how much it hurt Captain Kline because I felt I was right and he was wrong. I had slaved for him for two years, and he had not fulfilled his promise. My loss was his problem because he didn't do what he said. You see, orphans blame-shift and justify their actions, no matter how hurtful. Out of a selfish and distorted sense of being "right," they rationalize away all the hurt and pain they bring to others by demeaning them and criticizing them and questioning their motives.

As a newly appointed captain I went right to sea, and that very first week, out of about a dozen commercial boats operating from that port, I came home "top hook," meaning I had out-fished everyone else. This was a big deal because whoever was "top hook" in any given week was "the man." It came with a price though—I had to buy all the pints in the pub, but it was worth it. Being "top hook" meant I was now one of the best there was. My dream to be a top fishing boat captain had come to pass.

Week after week I came in as top hook. No one as young and as inexperienced as I was had become so successful so quickly. Someone might say, "Well, Jack, it sounds like you got your inheritance." Did I? But at what cost to my character and relationships? Where do you think I found all those fish? At the locations I had learned from Captain Kline. Like the prodigal son who valued his father only for what his father could do for him, I valued Captain Kline for what he could do for me.

Now I could walk into any of the waterfront bars and bask in the adulation of being one of the best in the business. I had usurped Captain Kline in that position, and he now sat alone in a corner of the bar, his head bowed over his beer, while his "bastard" son rose to glory. Oh yes, I became known as one of the top commercial snapper/grouper fisherman on the southeast coast of the United States, but what a high price I paid.

My orphan heart wasn't able to value relationships above inheritance. I wasn't able to feel compassion or empathy. My life was completely self-centered, self-consuming, and self-referential. I burned out many of Captain Kline's fishing spots, and while I was enjoying my rapid rise to success, he was in a decline because of a broken heart. My defection cost him dearly.

Reconciliation

Now Captain Kline wouldn't even speak to me in the bars or anywhere else. He would just look at me from over his pint, and etched into his face was the pain of my betrayal and of his broken heart. But in my orphan heart, I could not think of what I had done as betrayal. Captain Kline had served my needs, and I had moved on. Still I always felt grateful to him, and I remembered that I had once told him, "You're the first man who ever believed in me. You've given me something that no one has ever been willing to give me, and if I ever have a son, Captain Kline, I'll name him after you."

So, a year after I left Captain Kline, we named our firstborn son, Micah Kline Frost. With no children of his own, Captain Kline's name would have ended with him, and I wanted to honor the man who had done so much for me.

A few days after I sent Captain Kline a copy of the birth announcement, the phone rang. It was Captain Kline, who had hardly spoken to me for a year. "Jack," he said in a voice choking up with tears, "I just got the birth announcement. Would you go to breakfast with me tomorrow?"

"I'd love to, Captain Kline."

The next morning we met at the usual gathering place where all the fishermen meet. "Jack," Captain Kline said, his eyes glistening with tears, "thank you for keeping my family name going another generation."

I replied, "I'm going to do everything I can to keep your name in the Frost family line because I don't know who or where I would be without you."

Then he said, "Jack, would you forgive me for the way I've treated you the last year and for not rejoicing with you over your success?"

"I forgive you," I said. But it was 20 more years before I asked him to forgive me. It took me that long to understand how I had wronged him. Orphan hearts rarely feel the pain they cause others. They are unaware of the arrows they loose into other people's hearts. All they know is how "right" they are, and if someone else is hurting, that's their problem; they shouldn't have acted the way they did.

I thought I had received my inheritance when I left Captain Kline and went to work for a man who had never invested a day of his life or an ounce of himself into me. What I didn't realize was that a few years later, I would be radically born again, and a few years after that, I would leave the sea and go to Bible school. I went from making $50,000 a year fishing, to nothing.

After I stopped making a living at sea and went to Bible school, the boat owner I made tens of thousands of dollars a year for, never sent me a dollar in support. But Captain Kline has never stopped supporting our family. Through our friendship, his wife came to the Lord before she died, as well as Captain Kline. Today he still lives in the Daytona Beach area and loves to go down to the docks and hang out with the fishermen. He's a legend, and wherever he goes, he enjoys talking about a mate he once had.

"Have you ever heard of Jack Frost?" he'll ask a group of fishermen.

"Yeah, isn't he the guy who caught more snapper and grouper than anybody else? He was one of the best there ever was."

Then, beaming with pride, Captain Kline will say, "I taught him everything he knows."

"Didn't he leave the sea and go to preaching?"

"Yes," Captain Kline replies. "Let me tell you a story." Then he tells them of the drug-addicted, pornography-addicted alcoholic (like so many of them) who one day decided to go to sea alone for three days. "While out there, he cried out, 'Jesus, if You're real, prove it.' And from that time on, February 16, 1980, Jack was set free from drugs, porn, and alcohol. What Jesus did in Jack's life, He can do for you."

Without a heart of sonship, there is no legitimate inheritance. Captain Kline had an inheritance prepared for me, and he poured himself into me to make me ready for it. And I wanted it! But in the end, I didn't receive it legally because I was an orphan at heart, not a son. And only sons receive an inheritance. For two years, Captain Kline lived to meet my needs, and as long as he gave me what I wanted, I was right there: "How can I help you, Captain Kline? What can I do for you?"

But the moment Captain Kline had a need, as soon as he no longer met my needs but had to meet his own needs, I failed the test of sonship. That's when the true spirit that was in me was revealed. I closed my heart to him and abandoned him in the midst of his despair over his wife's illness and the financial problems it was creating. I valued what Captain Kline could do for me more than I valued relationship because I was not submitted to the father's mission.

Still, someone might be tempted to say, "Well, Jack, you got your inheritance anyway. You took what Captain Kline taught you and immediately became top hook. You gained a reputation as being the best. It doesn't sound like you lost."

But I did lose. If I had stayed with Captain Kline and waited for my inheritance, the income I would have received as captain and eventual owner of the fleet would have paid for my Bible school education and sustained my family for years to come. Instead, five years later, I wasn't making $50,000 a year anymore; I was in Bible school with no income for two years and a growing family. Because I was not subject to the father's mission, I chose short-term increase over the glory that would have come if I had waited for my inheritance. We ended up enduring 15 years of poverty in Bible school and in ministry during which I could barely feed my family. I gave away a million-dollar inheritance for short-term—and fleeting—satisfaction.

Paul says in Romans, *"For I consider that sufferings of this present time are not worthy to be compared with the glory that is to be revealed to us"* (Rom. 8:18 NAS). Inheritance comes only after enduring the "sufferings of this present time." Part of that suffering is patient obedience—being subject to Father's mission rather than our own. No matter how hard the present seems to be, and regardless of how difficult it seems sometimes to wait, nothing can compare with the glory of the inheritance that will be ours if we are willing to wait for it to come in our Father's good time.

But that inheritance is for sons and daughters. No sonship, no inheritance. Orphans don't possess the maturity for it; neither can they be trusted with it. The suffering of obedience builds character. Sons and daughters recognize the value of being subject to Father's mission...and of waiting for their full inheritance.

CHAPTER FIVE

RECEIVING YOUR INHERITANCE

The father of a friend of mine bought an old, antique, wooden, 18-foot speedboat when Peter was a teenager. His dad was prosperous, a member of the yacht club, and wanted to showcase the boat before all his boating buddies. He soon took the old teak boat to a boatyard and asked them to spare no expense in restoring it to mint condition. It took months of painstaking labor to refinish all the wood; install new fittings, chrome, seats, and cushions; remove the old 100-horsepower inboard engine; and install a new one with 400 horsepower.

Upon completion, it appeared to be a work of art, and the father could not wait to show it off to all his friends at the yacht club. In addition, he bought a brand-new trailer to transport the boat and a brand-new Jeep to tow the trailer. Then on a Saturday during the middle of lunch hour when all his buddies were eating at the yacht club restaurant, father and son drove to the launch ramp and lowered the priceless antique into the water in front of all his friends.

A number of his cronies came over and with envy pleaded with him to take them on a trial run out onto the river, but the father reserved the honor for him and his son. He took off from the yacht club full throttle and did a few spins back and forth for all to see as he gloated over his prized possession. Then he came racing back to the dock in front of the restaurant, and at the last second threw the gear in reverse at high rpm's, easing the boat to a stop. However, the force of revving up so much horsepower created a loud thud and water began pouring in from the stern (rear) of the boat.

Screaming at his son and friends to help bail out the water, he ran to get his new Jeep and trailer before the boat sank. Upon pulling the boat out of the water and inspecting the bottom, they found a huge hole in the keel at the stern. The exterior of the 50-year-old wood was varnished and looked like new, but the wood on the inside had dry-rotted during the many years, giving way to the pressures of the high-powered engine. Humiliated in front of his friends, the father's anger toward the workers at the boatyard exploded with verbal curses and accusation. Enraged, he commanded his son into the Jeep, jumped in, and sped off toward the boatyard to give them a piece of his mind.

In the meantime, blinded by his temper and embarrassment, he had forgotten to strap the boat down to the trailer, and as he was speeding down the road, a person in a car in front of him suddenly slammed on his brakes. When the father slammed on his, the boat slid forward off the new trailer, went through the back window of the new Jeep, and left the bow of the boat sitting in the driver's seat. The boat was destroyed, the new boat trailer mangled, and the new Jeep had sustained thousands of dollars worth of damages.

The moral of the story and of this chapter—*If you have not dealt with the dry rot in your life, and God turns up the power, you are in danger of blowing your rear end off!*

Taking Your Inheritance

There is a lot of teaching in some quarters of the church today about claiming or taking your inheritance—that your inheritance from God is your right in Christ, and you just need to reach out and take hold of it. There is truth in this reality, but it is not that simple. "Taking" your inheritance and "receiving" it are two different things that can produce two very different results.

Teaching on our inheritance in Christ is important. Many Christians don't really know who they are or what they have in Christ because no one has ever taught them. Inheritance teaching does address a legitimate and serious need within the Body of Christ, but the "take your inheritance now" emphasis can be easily misleading or misunderstood. An inheritance taken by an orphan heart with orphan thinking is in danger of blowing his rear end off. If we have not embraced healthy accountability relationships, the anointing can quickly empower us and take us places where our character may not be able to keep our boat afloat.

What parents in their right mind would release a $1 million inheritance to a 21-year-old son or daughter who is a drug or alcohol addict or who is immature and irresponsible in behavior? Rather, they would be wise to put the inheritance in a trust fund to be released when the child demonstrates the maturity needed to handle his inheritance in a responsible manner.

A premature inheritance almost always ends up in waste. Remember what happened to the prodigal son. He took his inheritance early, and as Jesus said in Luke 15:13, quickly "squandered his estate in loose living." Why? Because his character was not mature enough to take responsibility for his father's mission. The prodigal son was an orphan at heart, and his orphan thinking was not yet responsible enough to be a wise manager of the inheritance.

In the same way, when we insist on taking our inheritance *now* instead of waiting until we grow into maturity and allowing our Father to give it to us freely, we may end up consuming the blessings of God upon our own lusts. That's what happened to me when I left Captain Kline to work for the man who promised to make me captain right away. Because I valued the inheritance more than relationship, I left behind a trail of broken relationships. My orphan heart was too immature to appreciate fully the value of accountability and covenant relationships.

Here are a few characteristics of immaturity. Notice how each one also reflects characteristics of an orphan heart:

1. Immaturity is a slave to circumstances and emotions. Our circumstances determine whether we have a "good hair day" or "bad hair day."

2. Immaturity is a slave to self, seeking to meet personal needs at others' expense.

3. Immaturity seeks the place of comfort, ease, least resistance, and whatever makes us feel valued and affirmed.

4. Immaturity obeys out of a fear of loss or punishment, not because we do not want to grieve the one we love.

5. Immaturity values people for what they can do for us, not for relationship. Thus, we unconsciously use and manipulate people to meet our needs.

6. Immaturity demands its own way or nothing. "If you do not play my way, I am going to take my ball and go home."

7. Immaturity is subject to its own mission. Our thoughts continually gravitate toward me, myself, and I.

8. Immaturity is "obtain-oriented": "How does this benefit me?" Our choices are influenced by what we can gain.

9. Immaturity is self-centered, self-consuming, and self-referential. "Let's talk about you for a while...have you read my book yet?"

Paul says that as Christians *"we are children of God, and if children, heirs also, heirs of God and fellow heirs with Christ"* (Rom. 8:16b-17a NAS). "Children" here is *teknon* in Greek, the word for an immature child. Even as immature children, then, we are heirs of God and fellow heirs with Christ. This means that the fullness of Christ—everything we see in Him—is our inheritance. It all belongs to us. But that does not mean that we are supposed to get it all right now. In Galatians 4:1-7, Paul describes how a young child is an heir to everything yet does not actually assume ownership until the time set by the father. And until that time, the child can often feel more like a slave than an heir.

In the culture of Paul's day, a son was under the care and authority of tutors until he reached the age of 12, at which time he became apprenticed to his father. For the next 18 years, until the age of 30, the son worked as his father's apprentice, learning from his father everything about the family business or trade. Unlike the hired workers who received regular wages, the son often received no pay during his apprenticeship. Why? Because everything was provided for him by his father. He was still living in his father's house under his father's authority and care. His "pay" was learning from his father all the skills and trade secrets of their profession. Hired hands received wages, but the son was heir to the business. He had to wait, to "suffer" through his time of apprenticeship until he was responsible and mature in his knowledge and understanding of his father's business.

Normally, at the age of 30, the son completed his apprenticeship and was ready to receive his inheritance. At that time, if the son had proven himself faithful and remained in patient submission as a son subject to his father's mission, his father would buy or build him a house and establish him in his own business, where he would be set for life. As a child, the inheritance was always his, but first he had to show himself faithful with what his father had put into his hands. Jesus said that those who are faithful with a little will be put in charge of much (see Matt. 25:21).

Receiving our inheritance means first "suffering" by being faithful with little as we learn to take responsibility for much and being subject to Father's mission. Then our character is ready to handle God turning up the power.

Jesus Learned Obedience Through Suffering

Before we receive our inheritance in Christ as fellow heirs with Him, we first suffer with Him. Paul said that we are children of God, heirs of God, and fellow heirs with Christ. Continuing with the rest of that verse and the verse following, he says: "...*if indeed we suffer with Him so that we may also be glorified with Him. For I consider that the sufferings of this present time are not worthy to be compared with the glory that is to be revealed to us*" (Rom. 8:17-18 NAS).

Full entry into our inheritance as heirs with Christ involves suffering with Him for the greater glory to come. And how did Jesus suffer? Most of us think immediately of His suffering on the Cross, and that is certainly correct. However, only Jesus could die on the Cross for our sins. The only way we can suffer with Him in that way is in the figurative sense of "dying" to self and taking up our cross daily and following Him (see Luke 9:23)—in other words, dealing with the interior dry rot (motives) and not just having an attractive exterior. We begin to displace being subject to our own mission and seek to become committed to His mission. Paul described it this way: "*I have been crucified with Christ; and it is no longer I who live, but Christ lives in me; and the life which I now live in the flesh I live by faith in the Son of God, who loved me and gave Himself up for me*" (Gal. 2:20 NAS). Paul had come to a defining moment in life where he chose to be subject to Father's mission, and no longer his own, even if it was uncomfortable for him.

Jesus suffered on the Cross, but there is more involved with His suffering than just the Cross. Through His suffering, Jesus learned obedience—willing submission to the mission of others, especially His Father. The Cross was the ultimate demonstration of His submissive obedience. A companion passage to Romans 8:17-18 is Hebrews 5:7-9:

> *In the days of His flesh, He offered up both prayers and supplications with loud crying and tears to the One able to save Him from death, and He was heard because of His piety. Although He was a Son, He learned obedience from the things which He suffered. And having been made perfect, He became to all those who obey Him the source of eternal salvation* (Hebrews 5:7-9 NAS).

Even Jesus had to go through "the sufferings of this present time." He had to learn the whole walk of sonship because, once His public ministry began, the enemy was going to do everything possible to get Him to think like an orphan. A lot was riding on this. If satan could succeed in deceiving Jesus into orphan thinking, then Jesus never could be our Savior because He would become subject to satan's mission rather than His Father's. None of us then could be saved; none of us could experience the fullness of Father's love or of His gifts in our lives. Before Jesus could become the source of eternal salvation, He had to learn the obedience of a son and walk in a spirit of sonship.

In the same way, our gifts and calling are in danger of blowing our rear end off until we learn obedience from what we suffer as spiritual sons and daughters to someone. Whose son are you? Whose daughter are you? Do you value people for relationship or for what they can do for you?

Jesus Was Subject to His Earthly Parents

How did Jesus learn obedience? First, by being in submission to his earthly parents and then to His heavenly Father. In his childhood years, Jesus learned to love, obey, honor, and respect His earthly parents. A major shift began to occur when Jesus visited the Temple in Jerusalem at the age of 12 and culminated with the inauguration of His public ministry 18 years later at the age of 30. This period coincides with the time Jesus would have been apprenticed to His earthly father, Joseph, in the carpenter shop. His honor and submission to His earthly father was part of the apprenticeship to His heavenly Father and part of being subject to His mission.

Luke tells us that when Jesus was 12, He, Mary, and Joseph traveled to Jerusalem for the Passover, as was their custom. Starting home after the weeklong festival, Mary and Joseph assumed Jesus was somewhere in the caravan with friends or relatives, and traveled for an entire day before missing Him. Unknown to them, Jesus had stayed behind in Jerusalem. After they discovered He was not with them, Mary and Joseph returned to the city to look for Him.

Then, after three days they found Him in the temple, sitting in the midst of the teachers, both listening to them and asking them questions. And all who heard Him were amazed at His understanding and His answers. When they saw Him, they were astonished; and His mother said to Him, "Son, why have

You treated us this way? Behold, Your father and I have been anxiously looking for You." And He said to them, "Why is it that you were looking for Me? Did you not know that I had to be in My Father's house?" But they did not understand the statement which He had made to them. And He went down with them and came to Nazareth, and He continued in subjection to them; and His mother treasured all these things in her heart. And Jesus kept increasing in wisdom and stature, and in favor with God and men (Luke 2:46-52 NAS).

After three days of probably frantic searching and inquiries, Mary and Joseph found Jesus in the Temple, sitting with the teachers. No doubt those teachers had never had a boy of such understanding, wisdom, and insight in their midst before! Even in this setting, Jesus was in subjection as a son. He was the Son of God, yet He took on the role of a learner, listening and asking questions.

The Scripture says that Mary and Joseph were astonished when they saw Jesus. But they did not grasp the significance of what was happening. Instead, they scolded Him for making them so anxious concerning His whereabouts. Jesus' answer was simplicity and innocence itself: *"Did you not know that I had to be in My Father's house?"* Some Bible versions translate the verse, *"Did you not know that I had to be about My Father's business?"* Jesus was in training for His Father's mission—the mission of announcing and ushering in the Kingdom of Heaven and introducing people to the Father's love.

Apparently, Jesus' parents did not know; they did not understand what He meant. They took Him back home with them to Nazareth where He *"continued in subjection to them."* Jesus learned obedience "from the things which He suffered." We usually think of suffering as experiencing something painful or unpleasant, but the word also means to endure, to tolerate, or to put up with something. By "suffering" His parents' authority until He was 30, Jesus learned obedience. He was an obedient, faithful son to His earthly parents. He knew that in order to enter into His inheritance with His heavenly Father, He first had to be a son to His earthly parents. Then, at age 30, Jesus would be ready to be released fully into the work for which His Father had sent Him to earth.

Jesus Received the Favor of His Heavenly Father

Whenever we accuse or judge our earthly parents for any reason—abuse, indifference, lack of understanding and empathy, failure to accurately model the love of Father God, or whatever—we reject the spirit of sonship and become subject to our own mission in life. Later in life, this can become the dry rot that can sink our vessel. Jesus knew He couldn't go that route. He knew that the first step to being subject to His heavenly Father was to learn to be subject to His earthly parents. The result was that Jesus grew "in wisdom and stature, and in favor with God and men."

Favor with God is preceded by faithful submission (being underneath and dependent) to earthly parental authority. For 30 years, Jesus was subject to His mother and father even though they did not have nearly as much spiritual insight and wisdom as He did. For 18 years, He labored in the carpenter shop, learning the trade and assisting His father in various carpentry projects to help support the family. He suffered patiently in waiting and working in His father's house in spite of the anointing, gift, and call of Father God on His life. For 18 years, He postponed His own ministry in order to be in subjection to His earthly father; for if He could not be subject to Joseph's mission, neither could He be subject to Father God's mission. Death to self-centeredness, self-consumption, and to being self-referential begins to occur when we become subject to someone else's mission.

Now, at 30 years old, the time appointed by the Father had come, and Jesus was ready to move from slavery to sonship. The favor of God was upon Him, a fact demonstrated by another significant event in Jesus' life.

> *Then Jesus arrived from Galilee at the Jordan coming to John, to be baptized by him. But John tried to prevent Him, saying, "I have need to be baptized by You, and do You come to me?" But Jesus answering said to him, "Permit it at this time; for in this way it is fitting for us to fulfill all righteousness." Then he permitted Him. After being baptized, Jesus came up immediately from the water; and behold, the heavens were opened, and He saw the Spirit of God descending as a dove and lighting on Him, and behold, a voice out of the heavens said, "This is My beloved Son, in whom I am well-pleased"* (Matthew 3:13-17 NAS).

John knew he was not worthy to baptize Jesus because to do so would put him in a place of spiritual authority over someone greater than he. In another place, John confessed that he was not worthy even to untie Jesus' sandals (see John 1:27)—a menial task for the lowliest household slave. Yet Jesus insisted that John baptize Him. He continued to subject Himself to the spiritual authority of someone inferior to Him. He submitted to the spiritual authority of one whom God was using at the time to bring revelation and repentance to Israel. Jesus' submission was part of His spirit of sonship. He would not allow dry rot to enter His soul.

One characteristic of a son (or daughter) is a teachable spirit, a willingness to receive and learn from others even if they are less skilled or knowledgeable. Virtually everyone has something to teach the person who is willing to learn. Learning is the key to continuing growth throughout life. Those who stop learning stop growing, and those who stop growing start drying up while dry rot sets in.

People sometimes say to me, "Jack, you have an international ministry; you have counseled and helped bring healing and deliverance to thousands around the world. Why do you continue to position yourself frequently to receive ministry? Why do you still sit under others for prophetic prayer ministry and for marriage and family counseling?"

The answer is simple. How can I minister to others what I am not willing to receive myself? I have learned that I cannot effectively breathe life into others that which I am not willing to get underneath in humility and submission and receive for myself.

Humble subjection before God begins with humble subjection before legitimate human authority. John says that *"anyone who does not love his brother, whom he has seen, cannot love God, whom he has not seen"* (1 John 4:20b) A funny thing about love—you can't receive it without humbly submitting to it. Love always involves humility and submission. To paraphrase John, then: How can we have a heart of submission to God, whom we can't see, if we don't have a heart of submission to man, whom we can see?

Jesus understood this connection. He knew that part of His submission to His heavenly Father was to be in submission to His earthly parents and, in the case of His baptism, His cousin John. That's why He told John, *"Permit it at this time; for in this way it is fitting for us to fulfill all righteousness."* Because Jesus was subject and obedient as a son to legitimate earthly authority, He received powerful affirmation of the favor of His heavenly Father. The heavens opened, the Holy Spirit descended like a dove, and a voice from Heaven said, *"This is My beloved Son, in whom I am well-pleased."*

Jesus Endured a "Dry Season" in the Wilderness

The process of Jesus' life toward entering His inheritance and becoming the source of eternal salvation illustrates the sequence of the Great Commandment preceding the Great Commission. First, at His baptism, He experienced the expressed love and favor of His

Father, and then He was released to ministry. So often today we reverse the process—we seek release into ministry hoping to find God's favor by what we do or achieve. This process characterizes orphan thinking and can easily turn to dry rot.

Assured by the favor of His Father on His life, Jesus had one further test, one further training ground before He was released fully into His ministry—He had to endure a "dry season" in the wilderness. When we first receive the experiential revelation of Father's love, it seems that His love is the only love and affirmation we receive for a season, while many of the support structures that have been comforting us and feeding our need for attention and identity are ripped out from under us. Dry seasons help us discover whether or not we truly believe that Father's love is really all we need, so the Holy Spirit leads us into a wilderness season. Here the enemy will try his hardest to steal from us our spirit of sonship by enticing us with orphan thinking and counterfeit affections. This is exactly the tactic he took with Jesus:

> *Jesus, full of the Holy Spirit, returned from the Jordan and was led around by the Spirit in the wilderness for forty days, being tempted by the devil. And He ate nothing during those days, and when they had ended, He became hungry. And the devil said to Him, "If You are the Son of God, tell this stone to become bread." And Jesus answered him, "It is written, 'Man shall not live on bread alone.'"*

> *And he led Him up and showed Him all the kingdoms of the world in a moment of time. And the devil said to Him, "I will give You all this domain and its glory; for it has been handed over to me, and I give it to whomever I wish. Therefore if You worship before me, it shall all be Yours." Jesus answered him, "It is written, 'You shall worship the Lord your God and serve Him only.'" And he led Him to Jerusalem and had Him stand on the pinnacle of the temple, and said to Him, "If You are the Son of*

*God, throw Yourself down from here; for it is written, 'He will
command His angels concerning You to guard You,' and, 'On
their hands they will bear You up, so that You will not strike
Your foot against a stone.'" And Jesus answered and said to him,
"It is said, 'You shall not put the Lord your God to the test.'"
When the devil had finished every temptation, he left Him until
an opportune time* (Luke 4:1-13 NAS).

Just as he had done with Adam and Eve, satan tried to create
doubt in Jesus' mind about the integrity of God and His Word. He
began by appealing to the passions of the flesh and enticed Jesus
with the idea of focusing on meeting His own personal needs. After
40 days of fasting, Jesus was hungry, so satan suggested that He
turn a stone into bread. Jesus responded that there was more to life
than food.

Satan's next tactic was to try to coax Jesus into abandoning His
Father's mission by promising Him wealth, power, and influence
without having to work for them. All Jesus had to do was become
subject to satan's mission. Jesus refused, saying that God alone was
to be worshiped and served.

Finally, satan appealed to the "shortcut" spirit of the orphan
heart by tempting Jesus to take the easy way to winning the
acclaim of men. If he would jump from the roof of the Temple,
angels would save Him from death and everybody would acknowledge that He was the Son of God. Jesus refused again, saying it was
wrong to presume upon God.

Three times Jesus was tempted, and three times He resisted
orphan thinking. Through it all, He maintained His identity as a
son and remained faithful to His Father's mission. Jesus passed the
test of sonship and was ready to be released into His ministry. He
was ready to receive His inheritance.

Through the Suffering of Obedience, Jesus Received His Inheritance

Luke 4:14 says that Jesus returned from the wilderness *"in the power of the Spirit"* and began teaching in the synagogues. His time had come; His ministry had begun. One Sabbath, speaking in the synagogue of Nazareth, His hometown, Jesus described His ministry in the words of the prophet Isaiah:

> *"The Spirit of the Lord is upon Me, because He anointed Me to preach the gospel to the poor. He has sent Me to proclaim release to the captives, and recovery of sight to the blind, to set free those who are oppressed, to proclaim the favorable year of the Lord"* (Luke 4:18-19 NAS).

It is important for us to understand the progression in Jesus' life from slavery to sonship and into His inheritance, because our progression is the same. Jesus' heart of sonship is the prototype for every person ever born. Whatever we see in Jesus is ours as well because we are fellow heirs with Him. He went to the Cross to make it possible for each of us to bear our own cross and to crucify self-love. Let's summarize this progression in Jesus' life:

1. Jesus submitted to the authority of His earthly parents. For 30 years, He willingly made Himself subject to their mission.

2. Jesus submitted to the spiritual authority of one who was less than He—John the Baptist.

3. God the Father affirmed Jesus in His Sonship after His baptism. *"This is My beloved Son, in whom I am well-pleased"* (Matt. 3:17b NAS).

4. Jesus endured and passed the wilderness test, which determined whether or not He would be subject to His

Father's mission. In the wilderness, Jesus did not focus upon the enemy or upon His own authority; He focused upon being a faithful son.

5. Through the power of the Holy Spirit, Jesus was equipped and released into His ministry and calling. He began to walk in the fullness of His heavenly Father's inheritance.

Notice that Jesus received affirmation of His Father's love and favor *before* He sought to overcome temptation in the wilderness. None of us can consistently overcome temptation either in life or in ministry without the revelation of how much Father loves us; sooner or later orphan thinking will wear us down. Many people in professional ministry succumb to sexually inappropriate behavior during their ministry. Few people who enter the ministry in their 20s in North America will retire from ministry; they burn out and leave the ministry, never to return. Most seminary graduates who go straight into the ministry leave within five years never to return again. What is the main reason for these statistics? Too many put the Great Commission ahead of the Great Commandment. They are released into ministry (or release themselves) before they are affirmed in sonship. The dry rot has never been removed, and when the power is turned up, it threatens to blow their rear end off and sink their ministry.

Whose son are you? Whose daughter are you? Whose mission are you subject to? Who are you getting underneath of and supporting? I'm not talking about living under abusive authority; I'm talking about a heart attitude. Are you a son? A daughter? Or do you still struggle with an orphan heart?

Don't be in a rush to take your inheritance now. For if you take it before you have learned to be a son or a daughter, you may simply waste it, consuming it on your own lusts. Be patient. Displace the orphan heart and embrace the spirit of sonship.

Humble yourself in subjection to parental and spiritual authority, learning obedience through the things you "suffer." Allow your heavenly Father to affirm you in His love and in your sonship. In His time—at the right time—He will release you into your destiny and *"the sufferings of this present time are not worthy to be compared with the glory that is to be revealed to us"* (Rom. 8:18b NAS).

CHAPTER SIX

ORPHAN OR SON

In previous chapters, we have seen a number of Bible verses that speak of "sons" or "sonship," whereas "daughters" are not listed in biblical times because only sons received the inheritance. We know today that in Christ there are no favorites; there is neither male nor female in the Spirit (see Gal. 3:28). If being a daughter, or the lack of reference to "daughters," has left you feeling slighted, that's OK—your day is coming. For all eternity, the men in your life who know Christ shall be called the Bride of Christ. So, it will all balance out in the long run. For the sake of brevity, in this chapter, we will be using "sons" in a generic term that also includes daughters.

So far, we've talked a lot about the orphan spirit and the spirit of sonship and how each of us is to move from being orphans who have closed off our hearts to love, to being sons and daughters secure in the love of Father God and able both to receive and give love to others. It is only in making this transition that we can enter into the inheritance Father God has prepared for us and which is rightfully ours as fellow heirs with Christ.

Somebody may ask, "But how do I know if I have the heart of an orphan or the heart of a son? How can I tell the difference?

What are the identifying characteristics?" These are good and valid questions because recognizing and acknowledging your orphan heart is the first thing necessary toward embracing sonship. In this brief chapter, I want to outline quickly 20 basic contrasts between the spirit of an orphan and the spirit of sonship. These contrasts are also found in more concise form in Appendix A. As you review these contrasting characteristics, think about them carefully with regard to your own life and ask yourself, "Which of these applies to me?" You may find that in some areas you have the heart of an orphan and in others the heart of a son.

1. Image of God

Orphans see God as a Master whom they must appease continually. They feel that they must pray more, read the Bible more, or work harder to earn God's notice and favor. They are often left with a feeling that there is something more they must do or put in order before God will be pleased with them. To an orphan, God is not just Master, but also a *taskmaster*.

Sons, on the other hand, see God as a loving Father who accepts them unconditionally. They know that unconditional love is never based upon the performance of the one receiving it but upon the nature of the One giving it. Therefore, they do not have to strive or act in any certain way to "earn" Father's love; in Christ He loves them anyway, fully and completely, just as they are.

2. Dependency

Orphans are independent and self-reliant. They depend upon their gifts, talents, intellect, and anointing. They are convinced that they cannot trust anyone else. If they want anything, they must get it for themselves. "If anything is going to get done right, I'll just have to do it myself!"

Sons are interdependent; they know they need the community of love that God and the Body of Christ offer. This interdependency allows them to be open for Father's love to flow through them to others. Sons also know they are completely dependent on their heavenly Father, just as Jesus was. *"The Son can do nothing of Himself, unless it is something He sees the Father doing; for whatever the Father does, these things the Son also does in like manner"* (John 5:19b NAS).

3. Theology

Orphans live by the love of law. Like the Pharisees of Jesus' day, orphans try to relate to God on the basis of adherence to laws, principles, rules, and regulations. Orphans value obedience more than relationship.

Sons, however, live by the law of love. They value truth, knowing that the greatest truth of all is living to receive Father's love and giving it away to the next person they meet. Sons understand the biblical truth that *"love is the fulfillment of the law"* (Rom. 13:10b).

4. Security

Orphans are insecure but usually become quite adept at covering their insecurity. They often strive to act right and do enough to please God and earn His blessings. Therefore, they rarely experience an inward peace and rest. Life for an orphan is often filled with uncertainty and fears of trusting, abandonment, and intimacy.

Sons, in contrast, are at peace and rest in Father's embrace. They know that their security in God does not depend on their behavior but is based on the grace of God and on the saving work that Jesus did on the Cross.

5. Need for Approval

The need for approval is universal; we all desire acceptance. Orphans, however, are addicted to and strive for the praise, approval, and acceptance of man. But these counterfeit affections will not satisfy and instead lead to the fear of failure and rejection, which pulls an orphan heart farther away from God.

Sons are not influenced by this turmoil and fear because they know that they are totally accepted in God's love and justified by His grace. They don't have to strive for approval because in Christ they already have it.

6. Motive for Service

Orphans serve out of a sense of need for personal achievement as they seek to impress God and others. This often takes the form of hyper-religious activity. Some orphans then become so tired or cynical with the struggle that they lose motivation for serving and end up in apathy.

Sons, on the other hand, joyfully serve out of a motivation driven by a deep sense of gratitude for God's unconditional love and acceptance. Orphans serve expecting something in return; sons serve out of love and are giving-oriented.

7. Motive Behind Christian Disciplines

While some orphans are apathetic and possess no motivation for observing Christian discipline, there are those who do pursue the Christian disciplines—prayer, Bible reading and study, fasting, etc.—out of a sense of duty and a hope of earning God's favor. They often evaluate how spiritual they and others are by how much time they spend each day in prayer and Bible reading and how often they fast. Many orphans can quote the Bible extensively and pray for hours at a time, yet have never known personally the affectionate love and acceptance of God. Jesus chastised the Pharisees: *"You search the Scriptures because you think that in them you have eternal life; it is these that testify about Me; and you are unwilling to come to Me so that you may have life"* (John 5:39-40 NAS). Because their motivation is wrong, orphans who practice the Christian disciplines easily miss the love and intimacy of God.

Sons find the Christian disciplines a pleasure and a delight rather than a duty. Those who receive a deep revelation of Father's love often discover that many of the things they used to do "religiously" either lose their importance or take on a whole new meaning for them. A new motivation of love replaces the old motivation of duty, obligation, and fear. For sons, all the things of the Spirit, including the Christian disciplines, become sources of joy and pleasure because love brings life where duty and the letter of the law bring death.

8. Motive for Purity

Orphans believe they *must* be holy to be accepted by God; they *must* be completely pure in order to win His favor and avoid His judgment and wrath. The only way they know to achieve in these areas is to work and strive for them. Therefore, they live with an increasing sense of guilt and shame over their continuing failure to achieve perfect purity and holiness.

Sons *want* to be holy out of love for their Father. It is natural for sons to take after their fathers; they want to be "just like Dad." Sons who are secure in their Father's love don't want anything to hinder their intimate relationship. They don't want to grieve Him; they just want to be a resting place for God's love and His presence. Unconditional love is a greater motivator for purity than fear and intimidation.

9. Self-image

Orphans generally possess a low self-image and an attitude of self-rejection, which results from comparing themselves to others and feeling that they come out on the short end of the stick. Others seem more blessed. Others seem more loved. Others seem to get all the breaks.

Sons feel positive and affirmed because they know how valuable and precious they are to their Father. No matter what they do or how many times they mess up, they know that Father loves them anyway. They can pick themselves up and keep going because, feeling secure in Father's love, they know that they can do or be anything.

10. Source of Comfort

Because they have shut a portion of their heart off from expressed love, orphans seek comfort in counterfeit affections: addictions, compulsions, escapism, busyness, hyper-religious activity, etc., believing that the busier they are, the happier they are and the more worthy they are of Father's love. And because they have an independent spirit and depend on themselves, orphans find a false sense of comfort in their own good works.

Sons find true comfort in times of quietness and solitude as they rest in Father's presence and love. They have discovered that once having tasted of that place of rest, everything that the world or religiosity has to offer pales in comparison. Nothing compares with the comfort and joy of a son basking in the unconditional love of His Father.

11. Peer Relationships

Orphans often relate to their peers through competition, rivalry, or jealousy toward others' success and position. They believe they have to fight and scramble for every advantage and desire. Orphans cannot genuinely rejoice over the success or advancement of others. They fear that if they are not "on top," they will not be valued or respected.

For sons, on the other hand, peer relationships are all about humility and unity as they honor and value others and sincerely rejoice in their blessings and success. Sons are secure in their own identity and position, and therefore need not fear the success or advancement of others.

12. Handling Others' Faults

Conflicts are an unavoidable and everyday part of life wherever people interact with one another. Therefore, effective conflict resolution is a vital part of healthy interpersonal relationships.

Orphans, being self-focused, generally resort to accusation and exposure of other people's faults—while denying or trying to hide their own. In an effort to make themselves look good, they attempt to make others look bad. They seek to build themselves up by tearing others down and destroy relationships with issues of control, criticalness, possessiveness, or the lack of respect and honor.

Sons are relationship-oriented. In love, they cover (not hide) others' faults as they seek to restore those individuals in a spirit of love and gentleness. *Covering* a fault is different from *covering up* a fault. Covering protects a person from humiliating and destructive exposure until the conflict or fault can be resolved. Covering up a fault is an effort to deceive, which is a sign of orphan thinking.

13. View of Authority

Because of the abuse and mistreatment they may have suffered at the hands of authority figures in their lives, orphans will see authority as a source of pain and are therefore suspicious of any other authority, except their own. They are distrustful of the motives of those in authority, whether at home, at work, at church, or anywhere else. This is due at least in part to their lack of a heart attitude of humility and submission. Orphans resent and fear suggestions that they should submit to anyone by getting underneath them and supporting them. They regard being subject to someone else's mission as nothing more than allowing themselves to be used by that person.

Sons, however, look at authority differently. Sons are respectful and honoring of legitimate authority, seeing authority figures as ministers of God for good in their lives. Another way of illustrating this contrast is to say that sons are *teachable*, but orphans are not.

14. View of Admonition

Orphans have difficulty receiving admonition, even godly admonition, because they have difficulty acknowledging when they are wrong. In their own minds, they *must* be right, so when admonition comes, they receive it as personal offense or rejection. To justify their conclusions, they focus on others' faults, blame other people, try to vindicate and justify themselves, become negative or accusatory, or close their spirits to the one trying to speak admonition into their life.

Sons receive admonition as a blessing and a need in their lives because it exposes faults and weaknesses that they may not be aware of. They seek to put these weaknesses to death before they become relationship-threatening problems. Even though admonition may first cause their fur to bristle, they recognize it as valuable correction and an opportunity for growth. Without growth, there is no maturity; and without maturity, there is no inheritance.

15. Expression of Love

Orphans are guarded and conditional in their expressions of love. Expressed love by an orphan is based on others' performance and agreement. Because orphans have closed their hearts to love, they neither know how to give unconditional love nor how to receive it.

For sons, love is open, transparent, and affectionate. They lay down their own agendas in order to meet the needs of others. Love for an orphan is built on the question, "What can you do for me?" while love for a son is built around the question, "What can I do for you?" Love for an orphan is self-love; love for a son is *self-less* love. It means showing affection or affirmation even when he doesn't feel like showing it, simply because he knows the other person is in need of it.

16. Sense of God's Presence

For orphans, God's presence, if they sense it at all, is conditional and distant. *If* everything goes all right, *if* they have a good day, if they feel they've appeased the Master, if they think they have dotted all their i's and crossed all their t's, *then* they may sense God's presence. But even then, He often seems far away because their hearts are closed to intimacy.

Sons enjoy the close and intimate presence of God because they know that His presence and nearness do not depend on their behavior. They have discovered that He is with them all the time, no matter how much they get off center of His love. All they have to do is stop, return to the center of their heart where God's love dwells, and He is always right there. Sons know from personal experience the truth of the Scripture that says, "*Never will I leave you; never will I forsake you*" (Heb. 13:5b). Orphans question whether God loves them; sons know that God is crazy about them.

17. Condition

Orphans are in bondage. They are slaves to their fear, their mistrust, their independence and self-reliance, their sense of self-righteousness and self-justification, and most of all, to their loneliness.

Sons, on the other hand, live in the condition of liberty. Love has set them free from fear, shame, humiliation, guilt, and the constant need to prove themselves. They are free not only to receive love, but also to give it away in abundance without running out. Sons are free to become everything their Father created them to be.

18. Position

Orphans live life as if they don't have a home. They feel like servants or slaves. Their spirit is unsettled because they are away from safe harbor and don't know how to get back. They are frozen in numb-numb-ville in the midst of the sea of fear. Nothing satisfies, nothing feels permanent, nowhere feels like home.

Sons are at rest and at peace in the safe harbor of their Father's love. Outside the harbor the sea may churn and the wind may blow, but inside all is calm in Father's embrace.

19. Vision

Orphans are fired by spiritual ambition. They earnestly desire some spiritual achievement or distinction and are willing to strive to achieve it. They desire to be seen and counted among the mature.

With sons there is no proving, no striving after position, power, or prestige. Instead, they are content simply to experience daily their Father's unconditional love and acceptance and then be sent as a representative of His love to family and others. Intimacy precedes fruitfulness.

20. Future

For orphans, the future, like many other things in life, is always uncertain. Their attitude is, "Fight for everything you can get!"

Because they have no inheritance, orphans must compete for what they want, depending solely on their own gifts and talents to control and manipulate circumstances in their favor. And because the future is uncertain, they are most interested in what benefits them *right now*.

Sons are willing to wait for their inheritance because they know that their future is as bright as it is certain. As sons of a loving Father with infinite resources, they know they cannot lose and are willing to suffer now for the glory that lies ahead. Sons know that sonship releases inheritance, and they can patiently rest in their position as sons!

FINDING OUR WAY HOME

How do we begin to move toward God's perfect love so that we can displace the orphan heart? Remember that an orphan heart cannot be cast out; it must be displaced. It is a heart that does not feel like it has a home in a father or mother's embrace. Therefore, it is insecure with love and struggles with fears of trusting, rejection, and intimacy. Although we were created by Perfect Love so that we could receive His love and give it away, we became insecure with this unconditional love as a child. Insecurities and fears then filled the uncomforted areas of our heart. First John 4:18-19 infers that you cannot cast out these fears but you displace them by introducing the orphan to Perfect Love. Then the orphan must make a choice; he either risks opening up his heart and submits to love, or he continues to put up walls of self-protection and rejects love once more. *"There is no fear in love; but perfect love casts out fear, because fear involves punishment, and the one who fears is not perfected in love. We love, because He first loved us"* (1 John 4:18-19 NAS).

How do we begin movement from living life as if we don't have a home to living life as if we do? In the final four chapters of this book, I will present eight defining truths from my own journey that helped me begin displacing my orphan heart. These eight principles are the personal revelation that I needed in order to stop feeling like an orphan and start feeling secure and at rest as a favored son. Do not make the mistake of using these eight steps in a legalistic way or as a "formula." Everybody is different, and each person's approach to transformation will be unique to his or her particular situation.

The important thing here is not to mark off completed points on a checklist but to position your heart to come into alignment with Father's heart and away from the father of lies. This will require humility and a willingness to approach the whole process with the simple faith of a child. As Jesus said, *"Unless you are converted and become like children, you will not enter the kingdom of heaven. Whoever then humbles himself as this child, he is the greatest in the kingdom of heaven"* (Matt. 18:3-4 NAS). The Kingdom of Heaven is a kingdom of humility, innocence, and love; and only the child-like—those who are willing to humble themselves to become sons and daughters—will enter it. The depth of humility we embrace determines the depth of Kingdom life we will experience. These truths will take you on a path of humility—a willingness to be known for who you really are.

Truth #1 Forgive Your Parents for Misrepresenting Father's Love to You.

The process of moving from slavery to sonship begins with forgiveness. Specifically, it begins with forgiving your parents for the way they have misrepresented Father's love to you. Without forgiveness, there can be no progress. None of us are perfect parents, and none of us have had perfect parents. However, maybe your parents were great, and maybe you are not aware of any unforgiveness issues with them. If that's the case, that's wonderful; you are truly blessed. Let me encourage you, however, to examine your heart on this matter. Simply ask the Holy Spirit to reveal any pockets of anger, hurt, bitterness, disappointment, or disillusionment that may be hiding there over something your parents said or did to you—any place where you may have closed your heart to them. It doesn't have to be something "big." Sarah's perceived rejection by me when she was 5 was all it took for her to close her heart to me for 12 years.

If your childhood experiences with your parents were anything like mine, however, you may have several lingering issues. My mom and dad were pillars of the community and highly regarded in their fields. Dad was well loved and honored as a local club tennis professional, and Mom was one of the most highly respected teachers in the state of Florida, with a wall of plaques and other awards as testimony to her success in her profession. They were great people; they just did not know how to be a mom and a dad or how to express love, affection, and affirmation in their home life.

I endured verbal, emotional, and some physical abuse from my parents, brought on mostly by alcohol. I felt that nothing I did was ever good enough; all I did was disappoint them. As I mentioned before, by the age of 12, I had closed my heart to my parents. I became a rebellious and dishonoring teenager who also became addicted to drugs, alcohol, and pornography. When it came to forgiving my parents, I had a lot of issues.

The psalmist says: *"Forget your people and your father's house; then the king will desire your beauty. Because He is your Lord, bow down to Him"* (Ps. 45:10b-11 NAS). Forgiveness does not mean forgetting what your parents did, neither does it mean divorcing them in your heart. It means letting go of your identity of brokenness and dysfunction that you brought from your parents' house—an identity that is uncomfortable with love and keeps people at arm's length. It means taking up a new identity, the identity of a son or daughter in Father's Kingdom of love. And this is a deliberate choice that you can make right now. You don't have to wait.

The Kingdom of God is characterized by love, joy, peace, patience, kindness, goodness, faithfulness, gentleness, and self-control (see Gal. 5:22-23); this is our inheritance in Christ. We simply begin by focusing our life on what Jesus focused His life on—doing the will of His Father. Father God has commanded us to forgive, and forgiveness begins at home.

There was something inside me that wanted my parents to come to me and say, "Jack, forgive me for being a poor parent," and for them to specifically take ownership of the individual ways they hurt me. But in order for me to forgive my parents, it meant letting go of any expectation for them to make things right with me. Otherwise, it was as though I was reaching up for Father's love with one hand but keeping my other hand gripped tightly around my parents' throats until they made things right with me. Then I was caught in the middle, frozen in numb-numb-ville, and unable to move in any direction. Instead, I decided to let go of the blame I held against my parents. I chose to let them off the hook and give them a gift they didn't deserve—the gift of honor, understanding that they, like most parents, were probably also spiritual orphans possessing most of the orphan characteristics. They could not give to me what had never been given to them. (There is much more said about this in my book, *Experiencing Father's Embrace*, found in the chapters on "Father Issues" and "Mother Issues.")

Forgiving your earthly parents is critical to becoming a son or daughter; for when you rejected your natural parents, you also rejected the heart attitude of a son or daughter and became a spiritual orphan. Now, in order to displace that orphan thinking, you must be introduced (or reintroduced) to a loving Father. I'm not talking about re-bonding with your earthly mother and father necessarily; in many cases that may not be possible due to death or other circumstances. What I *am* talking about is letting go of the residual pain from life in your earthly parents' house so that you can reach up and receive God as your loving heavenly Father and trust Him to meet the deepest needs of your life.

Forgiveness does not guarantee healing. Forgiveness opens the door to healing, but forgiveness and healing are not the same thing. Why? Because forgiveness and trust are two different things. As an adult you may have prayed your heart out, gone through hundreds of hours of counseling, and done everything you know to do to forgive, even reaching a place of peace in knowing you have forgiven them; yet whenever anyone or anything reminds you of the offending parent, you get agitated or withdraw. You may have forgiven them, but you still don't fully trust them yet because you have not been fully healed. The important thing here is to begin movement toward sonship by forgiving.

In 1986, I began practicing forgiveness toward my parents after completing a lot of prayer counseling. I had been saved for six years and had graduated from Bible school. And even though I forgave Mom and Dad for all those years of torment, I still had a lot of anger, trust, and intimacy issues. I was still wounded and in pain. Forgiveness does not guarantee healing. Healing often calls for a more radical and more difficult but equally important step. In 1989, I began taking that step.

Truth #2. Ask Your Parents to Forgive You for the Way You Hurt or Disappointed Them.

Forgiving your parents is the first step toward sonship. But sometimes forgiving them is not enough to set you free. Depending on your particular circumstances, it may be necessary for you to seek forgiveness *from* your mother and/or father. It's easy to remember and rehash all the bad things they did and the way they mistreated you, but it's a lot harder to own up to all the ways you may have hurt or disappointed them. Many times the process of forgiveness calls for the ministry of restitution—offering restitution for your attitudes, behavior, and actions that have hurt others.

The ministry of restitution states that if our actions or attitudes have brought hurt to another person, there may be a need to go to that person and make right any wrong to break the destructive patterns in our relationships. Although God forgives us for each specific wrong the first time we ask, we may continue to reap what we have sown; so, in order to break that cycle and begin restoring trust, it is often necessary to make every effort to bring healing to others and to seek to restore the fractured relationship. Even if we feel the other person is 98 percent wrong and we are only 2 percent wrong, we are 100 percent responsible to walk in forgiveness and repentance for our 2 percent (see Matt. 5:22-26).

It may not be enough for another person to forgive you. You may still carry unconscious guilt or shame for the offense and have a need to ask for forgiveness to be free. There can also be a block in the relationship until you acknowledge to them that you have wronged them. The other person may have forgiven you, but their trust in you has been violated. Until you acknowledge your offense, it is difficult for them to trust you again because forgiveness and trust are two different things.

When I began dealing with the matter of forgiveness toward my parents in 1986, I knew I had many issues to resolve. As prayer counselors began helping me walk through those issues, God began restoring a degree of wholeness to my life. But I still had a long way to go.

The day finally came in 1989 when I realized, with the help of one of my counselors, that I needed to ask my parents to forgive me for everything I had put them through. At first I resisted. After all, with the pain I had experienced at their hands, why should I have to go to them for forgiveness? They ought to come to me! In my anger over the pain they had caused me, I was blinded to how much pain I had caused them.

From the time I was 12 years old, when I ceased being their son by closing my heart off to them, I treated them like dirt. Because my life was miserable, I wanted their lives to be miserable too. I did everything I could do to get revenge, to hurt them, to wound them, and to betray them.

And through all those years until 1989, I had never considered the pain this caused them. Orphans know only their own pain; they don't see the pain they inflict on others, or if they do realize it, they don't care because they feel that pain is justified. I didn't consider the pain I had brought to Captain Kline's heart, leaving him in the lurch when the situation no longer served my advantage. All I saw was my own disappointment, and that (at least in my own mind) justified my betrayal and my negative behavior.

One of my dad's greatest disappointments came the day I told him I was leaving the sea and going to Bible school. You should have seen the look he gave me! "With all the money you're making at the top of your business, you're giving it up to go to Bible school!?" He was a man who wanted nothing to do with church or with Christians. He had attended church as a boy, but only until he was seven because he had to. After his father abandoned him, everybody in the church rejected him because he was the only kid in town with no father. Dad had no use for the God I knew and represented, and for eight years after I was saved, he wouldn't let me talk to him about the Lord.

Reconciling With My Father

Despite all this baggage and background, when I resolved to approach my parents about forgiving me, I thought Dad would be easier to deal with than Mom, so I went to him first. I was 38 years old. At the time, he lived 400 miles away, and we saw each other only a couple times a year. We both liked golf, so one day when we were together on the golf course, I plunged in.

"Dad, I want to ask you to forgive me for the pain I put you through in my teenage years."

He stopped the golf cart, looked at me, and said, "What? Where did you get this crap from?"

I said, "Dad, at 12 years old, I closed my heart off to you and started treating you with all this resentment and anger. Dad, I want to ask you to forgive me." He just sat there stupefied. "Forgive me for the pain I put you through and for the times you came and bailed me out of jail, for the times you came to the hospital when I was overdosed on drugs. Dad, you don't know half the things I was involved in. I was a pornography addict and a drug addict. You don't know all the times I was taken into custody by the police and all the other things I've done wrong, but Jesus Christ has completely forgiven me. I realize how much pain I've caused you through the years, and I'm asking you to forgive me, because Jesus forgave me. Dad, please forgive me."

Dad was speechless. After about ten seconds, my dad said, "No, Son, I won't forgive you."

"Why, Dad? I really need you to look me in the eye and tell me you forgive me."

My dad who couldn't say the words "I love you," my dad who couldn't hold me, my dad who didn't want anything to do with God or any of this "religious stuff," my dad who never once apologized for the physical or emotional abuse, my dad who never acknowledged personal fault, my dad now over 70 years old, said, "I won't forgive you, Son, until you forgive me."

I was in shock. My dad started crying. He was a hard man who had never shed a tear, but now he was weeping. He continued, "You're asking me to forgive you when I'm the one who was so harsh and unmerciful. I'm the one who put you through hell on the tennis courts. You became what you became only because of how much I demeaned you, the way I screamed at you, and the names I called you. Jack, I never knew how to be tender with you; I never knew how to be kind. My dad left me when I was seven years old, and I was raised under harshness and anger and the shame of the community. I need to ask you to forgive me because I was angry that you didn't play tennis the way I wanted you to, and I took out all my agitations on you. I shamed you, I demeaned you, and I devalued you. Please, Jack, will you forgive me?"

For 38 years, I had never heard what I wanted and needed to hear my dad say. He had never apologized or in any way acknowledged the pain he had inflicted in my life. And now, for the first time, I heard an apology from him: "Would you forgive me?"

I thought, *Wow!* And I said, "Of course, I forgive you, Dad!"

As long as I was subject to my own mission—self-protection, blame-shifting, nursing my pain—nothing ever happened between Dad and me; nothing ever changed. But when I came to him and asked for his forgiveness, I became subject to Father God's mission—the ministry of reconciliation. And when I became subject to Father God's mission, I also became subject to my own earthly father. Every earthly father, no matter how much they've hurt their kids, longs for it to be made right. But many of them have no idea how to apologize. They don't know where to start.

My father never humbled himself to me until I first got underneath and was subject to his mission. Then he looked me in the eye and said, "Jack, I love you." It was the first time I heard him say that since I was 19 and in the hospital for a drug overdose, when he had come and embraced me and told me he loved me.

Now, on that golf course 19 years later, my father reached out, put his arms around me, and with tears in his eyes said, "Son, I love you. Thank you for forgiving me." And we cried together as we both asked forgiveness specifically and in detail for things we had done to each other. There was a lot of weeping, but oh, the joy! I experienced a homecoming and a dad with an open heart to me!

A year went by, and then one Sunday the phone rang. It was Dad. "Jack," he said, "I want you to know I went to church yesterday."

"What? You went to church?" I couldn't believe it. Dad had hardly been to church since his youth.

"It was a men's breakfast," he continued. "One of my old party-ing buddies came over to the house Friday night and said, 'I'm tak-ing you to church tomorrow.' I told him, 'I'm not going to church tomorrow.' He said, "Hey, I gave you free golf lessons, I trained you, I taught you everything you know. You owe me and I'm col-lecting the debt. Tomorrow, you're going to church with me.' I said, 'But there's no church on Saturday.' He said, 'It's a men's breakfast, and I'm the speaker.' 'You're speaking at church?' I asked. 'You were one of the biggest party animals in town!' He said, 'That was my other life.'

"So I went with him. At the end of the breakfast, he shared his testimony of recently accepting Christ at his wife's deathbed. Then the pastor prayed for those who didn't know Jesus to accept Jesus. Jack, I want you to know that yesterday I accepted Jesus as my Savior, but it wasn't because of anything my friend said at the breakfast. It was because a year ago you came and forgave me, and I realized that day that there must be a God. And when I looked at your life, I knew that only God could do in you what happened that day. That same day I started reading my mother's old Bible and have read it every day since. Ever since that day, I've just been wait-ing for the right moment to accept Him. It was your forgiving me that transformed my life."

Even after he was saved, my dad was never really keen on church because of all the personal pain he associated with it, but for the next ten years he was really keen on the love of God. He'd read his mother's Bible every day. Every phone call we had, he would tell me he loved me and that I was his hero. Dad is with the Lord now, but before he died, the two of us were completely reconciled. Everything was resolved. There was total closure. What peace that brings to my heart. It's truly amazing what can happen when you become subject to Father's mission.

Reconciling With My Mother

Having experienced such unexpected and complete success in being reconciled with Dad, I felt more optimistic about talking to Mom. So not long after that day on the golf course, I went to her and said, "Mom, I want to ask you to forgive me for all the pain that I put you through in my teenage years."

"It's about time you came to me," she snapped. "Do you know how much you hurt me?" She really lit into me.

Her angry, bitter response blew me away. No, I *didn't* know how much I had hurt her. At that time, I had not yet received the revelation of Father's love or entered into the spirit of sonship. I was still walking as an orphan, and orphans need everybody to say all the right things, or they put walls of protection up to keep people out. When Mom attacked me like that, I simply cut off the conversation. For the next ten years, I was very careful always to honor my mother in accordance with Paul's instructions in Ephesians: "*Honor your father and mother (which is the first commandment with a promise), so that it may be well with you, and that you may live long on the earth*" (Eph. 6:2-3 NAS). I was always polite and cordial. I honored her, but at the same time kept her at arm's length emotionally. My interaction with her was on a superficial level as I continued to protect myself from her criticalness and hurting me again.

Then in 1995, I received the revelation of Father's love and began learning to walk in that truth. Opportunities for ministry began opening up, and I moved also into teaching and leading conferences on Father's love.

In the summer of 1999, I was visiting Mom again, as I had every year. She and Dad divorced when I was a teenager and now lived five miles apart. Every Christmas and every summer I would drive the 400 miles home to see them, usually staying at Mom's house. One morning I got up early as I usually did, and hearing that I was up, Mom came out for the little verbal swordplay we engaged in every morning. She would try to get inside me, and I would try to keep her out: thrust, parry, thrust, parry. I loved her, I honored her, I blessed her, I sought to think good thoughts about her. I had even led her to the Lord in 1991. But I could not trust opening my heart up to her. So every time she tried to find an opening through my shell, I deflected her and kept things on a "safe" superficial level.

About this time, my dad walked in and rescued me, immediately saying all these wonderful things about how proud he was of me. For many years, this man had always pointed out everything I had done wrong, and now... I could do no wrong whatsoever in his eyes. For my part, as soon as Dad walked in the room, I lit up and came alive.

He had invited me to play golf with him, and as we got ready to leave, I glanced at Mom out of the corner of my eye. Although I noticed she was crying and wiping away tears, I still had an orphan heart to a degree, and it didn't register to me emotionally that I was the reason she was crying. I just wanted to escape. So Dad and I left.

A little later, after my wife got up, Mom asked her, "Why is it that Jack has such a wonderful relationship with his father, but when I try to have a conversation with him, it's like pulling teeth?"

Trisha, in her impeccable wisdom, said, "That's between you and your son. I'm not getting in the middle of it." Later, however, when we were driving home, Trisha told me about it. I just blew it off. I was honoring my mom to the best of my ability; what more did she want? I knew the Father's love but had not yet made the complete transition from orphan to son.

A few months later, in November, I spoke at a large international conference on the Father's love. It was the largest gathering I had been invited to, with over 3,000 people and some "top-tier" speakers attending. The size of the conference combined with anointed world leaders of such high caliber caused me to become so overwhelmed with insecurity that I was afraid I would not be able to minister effectively. By His grace, God blessed mightily anyway.

This circumstance raised my awareness, and I realized that even though I had been walking in a revelation of Father's love for four years, my understanding was still only skin deep. I was still more concerned with what people thought than with what God thought, and the key to deeper breakthrough and freedom continued to elude me.

The Missing Key

About two weeks later, during our "family reunion" (the yearly gathering of our team, intercessors, and supporters), the speaker, James Jordan, addressed the subject of the spirit of sonship and asked us the question, "When did you cease being your father and mother's son?" He went on to add, "When you rejected your mother and father, you rejected a spirit of sonship, and God will deal with you only as a son."

As soon as he said that, I knew I had found a missing key. I realized that I needed to go to my mother and ask her one more time to forgive me. To make sure I didn't chicken out, I told my wife my intentions. Mom would be visiting in a few weeks for Christmas, and I would talk to her then. I needed to practice the ministry of restitution with Mom because I was beginning to realize how much my attitudes had hurt her. I loved her, I had forgiven her to the greatest degree I knew how, and I practiced honoring her to the best of my ability. But something was still missing because my love was guarded around her.

I planned to talk to Mom the first night she was there, but I couldn't bring myself to do it. Or the next night, or the next. Finally, on the fifth and last night of her visit, I was getting ready to go to bed when Trisha confronted me. "Are you going to talk to your mother or not?"

Taking a deep breath I went to her and said, "Mom, I need to talk to you a minute." Here I was, a man of supposed faith and power, secure in Father's love, trembling in my mother's presence. I was scared to death.

We sat down in my study and I said, "Mom, this summer when I was home, and Dad came in and we had such a wonderful time together, I saw you crying out of the corner of my eye because Dad and I shared a depth of relationship that you and I have not possessed. Mom, I need to ask you to forgive me for the pain I have brought to your life through the years."

Immediately the sword thrusts began. "Do you know how much you've hurt me?"

"Yes, Mom, I know."

"You have done this to me since you were 12 years old, and I've never done anything to hurt you. How could you treat me like this?"

"Mom, I'm asking you to forgive me."

"I won't forgive you until you tell me what I've done wrong. I've been the perfect mother to you."

I couldn't believe what I had just heard. She went on about how she had been the perfect mother, never failing in any way to meet every need of my life.

I just sat there in shock. Ten years earlier I had shut down because I lacked basic trust in Father's love to meet my need when I was attacked. I had to justify myself, shift blame, and get the focus off me. My heart was closed. There was no revelation of Father's love. I was living life like a spiritual orphan.

This time it was different. I knew Father's love and was beginning to embrace a heart of sonship. I knew that I had to become subject to my mother's mission as a son and acknowledge how badly my closed heart had hurt her.

When I was about eight or ten years old, my mother and father stopped living together, even though they stayed in the same house. Dad moved into the furnace room and stopped speaking to my mother, and any communication between them passed through either my brother or me. Dad turned his attention to other things and people, and it destroyed my mother. She turned to bitterness and medicating her pain with alcohol.

As Dad poured every bit of his life into his oldest son, who was a real champion and one of the best youth league tennis players in the nation in those years, I spent all my time with my mother. I became her only source of sanity and love. But when I was 12, I had had enough and I closed my heart to her. This injured her even more because now all she knew was rejection and pain from every family member. From that time on, the criticism and the bitterness increased until every conversation over the next 36 years was a verbal sparring match. And for 36 years, I justified keeping her outside because of her negativism and criticism. I lacked the heart of sonship. I was subject to my own mission, rather than her mission or God's mission.

Sitting with her that night in 1999, listening to the familiar barrage and bitter tirade, I knew that Father would meet my need even as my mother was attacking me. Instead of shutting down, I felt something like waves of compassionate liquid love pouring over me, securing me in His love. Softly and gently I said, "Mom, this isn't about you; this is about me. I'm asking you to forgive me."

"I'll not forgive you until you tell me what I've done wrong."

"You don't know, Mom? You don't know?"

"I was the perfect mother. I've never done anything but love you."

That's when I realized that she really had no memory of the abuse I went through. Monday through Friday she was a teacher and sought to be a good mother. Although she was not a nurturer, at least she was there. She would come home on Fridays and all weekend long try to drink away the pain of being rejected by her husband and sons. And when she drank, she became violent, often venting her anger at her husband by taking it out on her sons. More than once, I found her covered in her own blood from self-inflicted falls or wounds.

"Mom," I said, "tell me one memory you have of one weekend from the time I was 8 until I was 18 and left home."

She couldn't. She had no memory of those weekends. She asked me what had happened, and when I told her of nights of being awakened and beaten for no reason, she said, "I don't believe it."

"Holy Spirit," I prayed silently, "please show her." I picked up the phone, handed it to her, and said, "Call your other son."

She wouldn't do it. Then she looked at me and asked, "Did those things really happen?" Right then the Holy Spirit dropped into her mind memories of her beating my brother and me. Suddenly, she started crying as memory after memory flowed. And for the first time she said through her tears, "Well, I did have an alcohol problem." Then she said the words I never thought I would hear her say to me: "Would you forgive me?" Just as with my father, this breakthrough with Mom did not come until I got underneath in submission to her as a son. Once I opened my heart to her again and dared to risk loving again, release came for her as well as for me.

That December day in 1999 I became my mother's hero. Her criticism turned to praise. This was a woman who, up until this time, had never apologized to me, never accepted blame for anything, and never even acknowledged her drinking problem. Now, for the first time in 36 years, I had a mother again. That's the power of forgiveness. That's the power of Father's love. That's the power of a heart of sonship. Last year, Mom also went to be with the Lord, and I am at peace in knowing that we had closure before she was promoted to glory.

Forgiveness is the first step in moving from slavery to sonship. Without it, it is difficult to take the next one. Who do you need to forgive? Who do you need to ask for forgiveness? Whose mission do you need to become subject to in order to bring healing, freedom, and release into your family and relationships? Do you think it would help your relationship if you went to your mom or dad and asked them to forgive you for the ways you have hurt or disappointed them?

(See Appendix B for further explanation on the ministry of restitution and how to approach someone and ask for their forgiveness.)

CHAPTER EIGHT

WHOSE SON ARE YOU?

Dealing with forgiveness issues covers the first two truths in our quest to move from slavery to sonship. Extending forgiveness (Truth #1) involves humility in laying aside our hurt and our perceived "right" to hold another person responsible for his or her offense against us. Seeking forgiveness (Truth #2) also involves humility, requiring us to lay aside our pride, acknowledge our sins and mistakes, and open our hearts to the one we have offended with no guarantee of being accepted. Humility makes us vulnerable and can sometimes be the difference between life and death.

The Devil's Hole

Barry was a friend of mine who I had gotten to know in our home church in the mid-1980s. He knew I was a licensed fishing boat captain and loved getting me to tell deep-sea fishing stories. One of Barry's longtime dreams was to catch a giant Warsaw grouper. In my years as a commercial fisherman, I had caught more giant grouper on hook and line than about any other fisherman on the East Coast. In fact, in the 1970s and '80s, I caught over

100 of these monstrous fish, which averaged about 175 pounds; ten were over 300 pounds, and one was a 450-pounder. To catch that one, I used a live 15-pound mahi mahi for bait, on a 300-pound test wire line.

In the early 1990s, Barry started to hound me, "Jack, will you take me out to catch one of those Warsaw grouper?"

There are several good spots for Warsaws right off Myrtle Beach, near where we live; one of them, Georgetown Hole, is 62 miles offshore. As commercial fishermen in the 1970s, we called that place the Devil's Hole because of the number of boats and fishermen who had disappeared without a trace while fishing there, including some friends of mine. Barry knew that I once had caught 28 grouper that totaled 5,000 pounds in one night at Devil's Hole. On another night I caught 14, and on still another, 9.

Barry finally persuaded me to go in the fall of 1991, a few years after I had left the sea and was no longer working full time as a boat captain. By that time, the giant Warsaw grouper had been classified as endangered on the East Coast and was illegal to fish for. So, any Warsaw we caught we would have to release, which rarely did much good. These fish come out of deep water and when brought up from 300-400 feet below, they often die from the pressure change. So I was already in violation of governmental authority, which was about to prove to be very unprofitable for both Barry and me.

Barry was and is a great guy, friend, and young man who really loves the Lord. But at that time and all his life up until that time, he had had a problem with abandonment and the results of it. His father had died suddenly when he was 8 years old, and he had never gotten beyond the rejection and shame he grew up in. Barry was a true orphan with most of the orphan characteristics listed in Chapter Six. The abandonment issue left Barry with a fear of trusting and a dislike for authority and anyone telling him what to do. He was independent and self-reliant and had never received revelation to the truth of submission to spiritual authority or authority at work. Barry was familiar with getting his own way and refusing to allow anyone to tell him what to do. With the orphan characteristics operating in his life, Barry was often right in the center of any discontent that occurred in the church or in his workplace.

The only boat I could find that any of my old fishing buddies would let us use was a 25-year-old, poorly maintained, 35-foot-long tub called the *Bronco*. Supposedly, the *Bronco* was a cursed boat; every person who had ever captained that boat had ended up divorced, bankrupt, or injured. It just sat at the dock; nobody would go near it. Fishermen as a whole are very superstitious, and they thought I was crazy to take it out. But for me, a curse without a cause can't land. After all, I was walking in Christ. I knew we'd be fine.

So, Barry and I loaded up enough gear for a three-day trip and headed out to Devil's Hole on the *Bronco*. The weather forecast was calling for mild winds and calm seas, and our outbound trip went fine. That first day we reached Devil's Hole and caught several hundred pounds of red snapper and grouper, and that night hooked up but broke off one giant Warsaw.

The next day, an unforecast low-pressure area began building off the coast. As the seas slowly built in height, Barry started turning a little green around the gills (seasick), and by nightfall, the wind velocity at Frying Pan Shoals light tower was 39 knots. The rest of the fishing fleet had returned to safe harbor, but I stubbornly remained trying to catch a Warsaw. We were 62 miles offshore; and by evening, seas began running about 12 feet, and here we were in this old 35-foot scow that seemed ready to fall apart.

This was Barry's first time out of sight of land. He was no seaman and ended up sprawled out on the back deck, puking his guts out from seasickness. He was as sick as he had ever been before in his life, so I finally relented to taking him home. Our course to safe harbor took us almost directly head-on into the 12-foot seas, so we were really taking a beating. I was in my element, locked into "captain mode" and having a great time. This was the kind of adventure I lived for! Meanwhile, Barry was on the back deck giving up everything within his stomach. He was definitely green, terrified, and wishing he had never come to sea with me.

I finally let Barry come into the wheelhouse once I was sure he had nothing left to up-chuck. While he rested on the bunk on the starboard side (right) of the wheelhouse, wracked with dry heaves, I steered and kept the spotlight shining off the bow onto the waves, so I could see when I needed to back off the throttle to endure the brunt of the larger waves that had no back side to them. I was running about five knots, trying to get us as close to land as possible where the waves weren't so brutal, but for 40 miles we were hammered with 12-foot waves pounding continuously into our bow.

"We're Going to Die!"

With over 2,000 days captaining vessels at sea, I knew the ocean well. I've lived there and weathered many storms, including 69 mile-per-hour winds with 20- to 30-foot seas in a 44-foot boat. I'm a survivor. So I knew which waves were the most dangerous.

In the early morning darkness, the spotlight now illuminated a rogue wave menacingly forming right off my bow. Every seaman's nightmare is the "rogue wave," often formed when two waves come together from an angle and converge into one, increasing their height by up to 50 percent and doubling in destructive power. Rogue waves are deadly and can take a boat to the ocean floor in seconds.

Terror threatened to overwhelm me as it rose to 18 to 20 feet and broke across the bow right into the face of the wheelhouse. There was nothing I could do but scream, "Rogue wave!" It smashed into us with such tremendous force that it shattered the safety glass in all three forward windows, tearing window framing loose from the fiberglass, and tearing off the starboard wall and windows from the wheelhouse. Shards of glass exploded into me from my neck down, ripping my shirt off. Blood was pouring from dozens of small lacerations, and a fragment of window framing was embedded in my throat and right arm. The impact of the wave threw Barry hard onto the deck, breaking or bruising several ribs and fingers. The wave had washed the antennas off the roof, drowned out our radio, and swept thousands of fragments of safety glass and debris into the engine room, clogging the bilge pumps that normally automatically pump any excess water overboard. We were still 22 miles from land and with the radio disabled, nobody knew where we were or that we were fighting for our lives.

Barry was in agony! I was in agony! And the boat was full of water. Stability was lost, and we were in a fight for our lives! I knew that if we stopped making headway and turned sideways into these heavy seas we would roll over and capsize. In the water, hypothermia would render us unconscious in a few minutes with death soon following—that is, if the sharks, attracted by so much of my blood in the water, didn't get us first.

Bleeding, wracked with pain, and struggling with every ounce of strength to keep the crippled boat on course, I screamed at Barry in full "Captain Bligh mode," "Barry, climb below into the engine room and unclog the pumps. We've got to get the water out of the boat!"

Barry, remember, is the guy who never liked anybody telling him what to do; everything had to be his idea. "I can't do it, Jack," he moaned as he rolled around on the deck in pain. "I'm too busted up."

"Barry!" I screamed louder, "I can't leave the wheel or we'll turn sideways to the waves and capsize! You've got to do everything I tell you to do or we will sink in a matter of minutes!"

"I can't do it! It hurts too much to move! Oh, it hurts…"

"BARRY, GET BELOW AND UNCLOG THOSE PUMPS *RIGHT NOW, OR WE ARE GOING TO DIE!!*"

I was injured more seriously than Barry, and it was all I could do with one good arm to keep the bow of the boat pointed into the seas. With all the excess water in the boat threatening to capsize us at any moment and with the bilge pumps clogged, Barry faced a choice—be subject to the captain's mission or die.

He could have justified doing nothing by blaming me for the trouble we were in and how poor my judgment was for keeping the boat at sea too long in heavy weather. But something finally clicked in Barry's brain. He comprehended the peril we were in and went beyond his and my brokenness and started listening to me. He jumped right in there to help as if a little voice had told him, "It's time for you to take on an attitude of sonship." Although in great pain from his own injuries, Barry followed every command exactly as I told him. He had his part to do, and I had mine if we were going to fulfill our mission—finding our way home.

Somehow Barry managed to get the engine room hatch off and went below, and with his hands and broken fingers dug shattered safety glass and other debris away from the bilge pumps. He filled buckets with trash, climbed back out of the engine room, threw it overboard, and climbed back in, repeating the process over and over. For the next two hours, Barry overcame his fears and pain in order to get the bilge pumps working again. Then, using the same buckets, he bailed water until the boat was empty and stability was restored.

With the immediate crisis over, I determined that it would be difficult to make headway in heavy seas without a windshield to block the water that often broke over the bow from the waves, so we anchored during the remaining few hours of darkness. Barry lay down in the back of the boat torn with pain and paralyzed with fear. I passed the night worshiping and singing in the Spirit in order to keep fear from consuming me. In all my years at sea, this was perhaps the closest to death I had ever come.

The next morning, the wind and seas eased up, and we limped into port. Barry was still in numb-numb-ville, frozen to the rear deck in fear. As we began to pull into the marina, fishermen at the docks saw the unbelievable damage to the *Bronco* and came running from every direction to help secure the dock lines. No one had ever seen a boat as mangled as ours come in under its own power. A later inspection revealed that the boat was not even worth salvaging but was junked. It truly was a miracle that Barry and I even survived.

From Slave to Son

As soon as we docked, Barry crawled on shore and got down on his hands and knees and kissed the ground. While I went to the hospital to get sewn up, Barry drove to our pastor's house. "Forgive me," he said to our pastor. "Forgive me for rebelling against you and stirring up discontent." Then on Sunday, he stood before the whole church and asked them to forgive him. As he lay on the deck through that long and terrifying night, he saw with crystal clarity how his whole life had been of independence, rebellion, and discontent. But that night on the deck of a crippled boat called the *Bronco*, he learned obedience by the things he suffered.

Barry had previously never been able to hold down a decent job, and he had always lived in poverty. After our close call at sea, however, he went back to work with a new spirit of sonship. He apologized to his boss for not making what was important to him important to Barry. In that first week, he led three people to Christ by telling them about our ordeal. Within a year, he was promoted to the safety manager over the plant because, instead of whining and complaining about everything he didn't like at work, he got underneath and supported his company and his boss, just like he had done with me that night on the raging sea. And Barry has grown and prospered financially and spiritually ever since. He became a man who lives to dispense gifts of honor and blessing to others. He moved from slavery to sonship.

The moral of the story from my point of view—don't take Jonah to sea with you. The moral from Barry's point of view—don't go fishing with someone who is more concerned with catching giant Warsaw than he is in maintaining healthy relationships.

What crisis will it take for you to begin movement from slavery to sonship? Why wait any longer? Perhaps today is a good day to talk to your pastor or prayer partner about your need for a home-coming in Father's love.

That brings us to truth #3 in our quest to be subject to Father's mission.

Truth #3. Focus Your Life Upon Being a Son or Daughter.

Now, the only subject Barry could talk about after we returned was how I had saved his life at sea in the bloodied and wounded state I was in. But it was his getting underneath me that saved my life as well as his. A heart of sonship recognizes its need for inter-dependence. So often, we see the bloodiness of our pastor or our boss and use their faults and weaknesses to justify our inaction instead of getting underneath, supporting, and saving both their lives and ours.

Sonship is a heart attitude of submission that brings self-redemption. When Barry and I were on that sinking boat, one of us had to submit to the other who was more knowledgeable and experienced in order for both of us to survive and overcome.

Somebody had to be a son. Somebody had to get underneath and push up. Somebody had to get his or her hands dirty, even if those hands were broken. Somebody had to lift up in support to ensure the success of our mission—to find our way home. And with the success, both of us survived, had a change of heart, prospered, and ended up with an adventurous story to tell.

In a gathering of like-minded ministers, most of whom had been mentored by Jack Winter, a 20-minute conversation revolved around Jack and his life as a spiritual father to many of us. During this time, he remained very quiet and seemingly uninterested, and finally he spoke up and said, "I do not want to be anyone's father. I want to focus my life upon what Jesus focused His life upon. Jesus focused His life upon being a son. Until I am more secure in being a son, I think I would just like to focus my life there."

He went on to say, "When you focus your life on being a leader, it becomes very easy to become controlling or authoritarian. That is characteristic of an orphan heart. Then you produce children after your kind. Instead, why don't we all start focusing on being a son or daughter who seeks to do only what the Father does, and lives to serve, honor, and bless others? When you do this, people around you will start living and acting like sons and daughters too."

Something in my heart sung out in agreement. "That is what I want! Who do I seek to honor and get underneath and push up, making their lives and ministry a blessing? Whose son am I?"

No one can be a father who has not first been a son. No one can be a mother who has not first been a daughter. Sonship begins in the natural before it moves to the spiritual because the natural precedes the spiritual according to Paul in First Corinthians 15:46. Before you can be a son or daughter in the spiritual, you must be one in the natural.

You do not come into your inheritance or become an effective influencer in the lives of others by focusing on being a leader or even by focusing on being a spiritual father. You come into maturity by focusing on being a son. That is what Jesus did. We saw in Chapter Five how Jesus focused on being a son the entire time He was on the earth, first as a son to His earthly parents, and then as the Son of His heavenly Father. Everything Jesus did and said was from the perspective and mind-set of a son. Jesus was the man He was, because of the Father He had. Whose son are you?

Scriptural support for this whole idea is found in Hebrews 13:17: *"Obey your leaders and submit to them, for they keep watch over your souls as those who will give an account. Let them do this with joy and not with grief, for this would be unprofitable for you"* (NAS). We must acknowledge our need to be a son or a daughter to someone else, or it will become unprofitable for us. If Barry had chosen the way of blame-shifting, fault-finding, and justifying (orphan thinking) in the midst of our crisis at sea, what would he have gained from that? Being right? Sure—being dead right!

What thoughts do you think arise in your pastor's mind when your name is mentioned? Would it be, *Oh, yes! Their heart is given to bringing honor and blessing to others!* or *Oh, no! What are they agitated and discontent with now?* How about your boss? Does your boss see you as someone who chooses to stoop underneath and push up, doing everything to honor him and make the business succeed, or does he or she seek to avoid you? It is your future that is at stake. What you reap in life next year is often determined by how the authority figures in your life see you right now. Are you an orphan with your own mission, or are you a son or daughter committed to their mission? Your future inheritance depends on whether you have a heart of sonship or an orphan heart. There is no inheritance for orphans. *"And if you have not been faithful in the use of that which is another's who will give you that which is your own?"* (Luke 16:12 NAS).

The Acid Test

The heart of sonship is a heart that has learned to *honor* all people! Blessings in life are promised if we honor our mother and father (see Eph. 6:1-3). Answered prayer and intimacy with God is promised to husbands who honor their wives (see 1 Pet. 3:7). Favor with God is found by honoring those in authority as well as honoring every person you come across (see 1 Pet. 2:17-20). Sonship, humility, submission, being subject to Father's mission— these character qualities are often interchangeable and are a natural manifestation of a heart that has had a personal revelation of honor.

Honor involves a decision that is made to put love into action, to give a person a position of high value and worth. Even when we have been disappointed, hurt, or wounded by a person, honor chooses to make a decision not to respond in kind. No matter what is felt coming from another person, honor chooses to not expose but speak words that give grace to the hearer. Honor views each person as a precious gift of God's creation and grants them a position that is worthy of great respect. Honor chooses not to respond with an unwholesome word or tone.

Not to give honor is to assign dishonor. Judgment, resentment, anger, exposure, sarcasm, criticism, comparisons, favoritism, jealousy, selfishness, envy, and racism are weapons of dishonor that are used against those who are considered of little value or worth.

Each time we have a point of contact or interaction with another person, we have a decision to make. We will either arm ourselves with a weapon of dishonor, or we will give an unmerited gift of honor. Have you noticed there's no middle ground? We can be 100 percent right in our evaluation of a person's faults or weaknesses or how they've disappointed us or how they have not matched up to our expectations, but love covers and does not expose others' weaknesses or whine about them.

What are we communicating when we talk to other people? Do people feel value and worth being spoken by us about those whom others may feel have little worth? Genuine sonship gives honor, while an orphan heart takes honor and dispenses dishonor. Not to honor can actually become a self-imposed curse and may result in a cloud or shadow of judgment hanging over our home, workplace, church, or relationships. Dishonor does not serve our personal interests and values, even if our judgment is accurate. It is unprofitable, and our inheritance in the Kingdom of God is delayed.

Probably my greatest pitfall in walking in honor is that I am often right in my evaluation of others' attitudes, behavior, and weaknesses and the way they have let me down or disappointed me. But is my body language covering or uncovering them? Is my conversation bringing exposure, or is it leading to restoration? When the name of someone who has disappointed me comes up in a conversation, do my words, tone, or body language bring honor, or do I draw out a weapon of dishonor? Is that person's redemption at the root of my words, or am I seeking to make myself look innocent by uncovering the fault? Honor is the acid test for a heart of sonship.

Some Christians have trouble focusing their life upon being a son or daughter because their past experiences with authority have been negative. But the sonship that we're talking about here really has little to do with authority in our life. It is an issue of honor. Sonship is not for the benefit of authority. Getting underneath and pushing up and being subject to another person's mission isn't about that person. It is about honor and whether or not you choose to be subject to Father's mission.

> *Submit yourselves for the Lord's sake to every human insti-*
> *tution, whether to a king as the one in authority, or to governors*
> *as sent by Him for the punishment of evildoers and the praise*
> *of those who do right. For such is the will of God that by doing*

right you may silence the ignorance of foolish men. Act as free men, and do not use your freedom as a covering for evil, but use it as bondslaves of God. Honor all people, love the brotherhood, fear God, honor the king (1 Peter 2:13-17 NAS).

I feel like one of the central themes of this whole discussion is found in verse 17 in the phrase, *"Honor all people."* A heart of submission is a heart that honors all people. Honor begins at home. Do you honor your spouse? Do you honor your children? Or do you inflict emotional pain on them with weapons of dishonor?

Do you honor the waitress at the restaurant and the checkout clerk at the grocery store? Do you honor the people who deliver your mail, pick up your garbage, or baby-sit your kids? Do you honor your coworkers, including those under your authority?

Do you honor the "little fish" who cross your path day by day? Or do you honor only the "big fish"? I never wanted my picture taken with little fish. They had no value. There wasn't enough meat on them worth eating, and their picture didn't give me bragging rights. But when I caught a big fish, I made sure I got a picture to show the world. There was plenty of meat to eat on the big fish, and there was money to be made from selling them.

If we give a gift of honor to the "big fish" who have the power to promote us or give us something we want, but we do not dispense gifts of honor to the "little fish," those we feel have no value to us, then the honor we give to the big fish is actually manipulation and control, as we try to get something we want from them. In other words, if we are nice to the person buying us lunch but not nice to the one serving us lunch, then we are not a nice person, and we lack a heart of honor, humility, and sonship.

Sonship is not something you measure only by the way you respond to those in authority—big fish. Sonship is also demonstrated by the attitude we exhibit toward the little fish—the clerk in Wal-mart at Christmastime, the person who cuts us off in rush-hour traffic, the family at home. At church, do you give out gifts of honor to the nursery or maintenance worker as much as you do to the pastor?

The call to sonship is a call to honor *all* people. But such a call is impossible to fulfill on our own. The only way to do so is to be subject to Father's mission—to submit to His love, and to look for ways to commit "senseless acts of humility and honor"—giving away gifts of God's love that are not meant to profit us. *"We love because He first loved us"* (1 John 4:19).

CHAPTER NINE

CLOSING OPEN DOORS

Every person on the face of the earth is a member of the "walk-ing wounded." There is not a single one of us who has not at one time or another been hurt by the words, actions, or indiffer-ence of another person. And all of us are guilty of inflicting wounds on others, most often those closest to us. We have criti-cized, demeaned, belittled, ridiculed, humiliated, intimidated, manipulated, controlled, exploited, or otherwise abused or mis-used others; and others have done the same to us. Sad to say, Christians can be just as guilty of this as anybody else. Church leaders can control or abuse their members, and church members verbally attack their leaders. Many of these wounds can last a life-time, like open sores that stubbornly refuse to heal. This is why the principles of forgiveness and restitution are so important in the process of moving from slavery to sonship.

As we saw in Chapter Seven, forgiveness and restitution begin at home by forgiving our parents for misrepresenting Father's love to us and by seeking their forgiveness for our rebellion and failure to honor them as sons and daughters. Learning to honor parental authority leads to the next logical step, which we discussed in the last chapter—recognizing our need to humble ourselves and to focus our life upon being a son or a daughter to someone who will be a mentor or spiritual father or mother to us. Whether our sonship is genuine can often best be measured by the honor or dishonor we dispense to the little fish in everyday life.

Moving into this stage of the process often awakens in us awareness of other problem areas that we may need to deal with if we don't want to become stalled by the *three basic fears*: the fear of *trusting*, the fear of *rejection* and *abandonment*, and the fear of *opening our heart to love*. Many of us have unresolved issues with authority figures beyond our parents—at home, at church, at work, and in the world. This awareness leads us to the fourth truth in our journey from slavery to sonship.

Truth #4. Forgive Spiritual and Governmental Authorities.

Is there any Christian who has never been hurt by church authority? Is there anyone who has never been taken advantage of by a boss, a coworker, or a friend? Unfortunately, that's life in a fallen world. There really never has been a universal revelation of Father's love on the earth. We've had a revelation of Jesus, a revelation of the Holy Spirit, and a revelation of power; and many ministries have been built upon the anointing of God, but few have been built upon a revelation of Father God's unconditional, affirming, and compassionate love. That is why in moving toward sonship, we must forgive governmental authorities, forgive our coworkers, and forgive those within the church who have hurt us, disappointed us, or misrepresented Father's love to us in the past.

Malachi 4:5-6 prophesies that in the endtime a fathering spirit will be released on the earth; but before there can be fathers, there must be sons, and before there can be mothers, there must be daughters. Those who embrace sonship today and "suffer" through the time of training and preparation for maturity, are the ones who will embody the fathering spirit on earth tomorrow. In the meantime, it is important to be willing to walk in a heart attitude of honor and submission to all legitimate earthly authority.

Paul makes this abundantly clear in the 13th chapter of Romans:

> *Every person is to be in subjection to the governing authorities. For there is no authority except from God, and those which exist are established by God. Therefore whoever resists authority has opposed the ordinance of God; and they who have opposed will receive condemnation upon themselves* (Romans 13:1-2 NAS).

There's that word "subjection" again, which means underneath and dependency. Who was Paul writing to? The Christians in Rome. He told the Roman believers to submit to the authority of the Roman government, a government rife with corruption, assassination, immorality, idolatry, brutality, destruction, and death. How could Paul call on followers of Christ to submit to such an ungodly system? I don't begin to understand, but I do know that Paul had a revelation of sonship. He understood the importance of believers having a heart attitude of humility, honor, servanthood, and submission.

Did the Christians subject themselves to everything the government decreed? No. Rome required that once a year every citizen and resident of the empire kneel before a statue of Caesar and declare, "Caesar is lord." It was a political loyalty test, and those who refused were regarded as traitors to the empire. Most Christians refused, acknowledging only one Lord—Jesus Christ. As a result, many believers were persecuted severely, and some were killed in the arena or executed. What Rome never understood was that the Christians who understood sonship, their refusal to bow to Caesar notwithstanding, were the most faithful, law-abiding, and productive subjects in the empire.

Giving the Enemy a Key to Your Front Door

With us, as with them, displacing the orphan heart begins in the natural by adopting the heart attitude of a son, not only toward our parents, but also toward all legitimate earthly authority, both governmental and spiritual. If we do not have the heart of sonship toward authorities in the natural realm, how will we ever have it toward God? As Paul says in these verses, all existing authority has been established by God; therefore, those who resist are opposing God and inviting condemnation on themselves. How can we be in sonship toward God if we are opposing Him?

This goes right along with Peter's instruction to "honor all people" that we looked at in the previous chapter. "All people" certainly includes those in authority. Peter continues in the very next verse: *"Servants, be submissive to your masters with all respect, not only to those who are good and gentle, but also to those who are unreasonable"* (1 Pet. 2:18 NAS). Unreasonable? It's easy to be in subjection to someone like Captain Kline, who was always there for me, who never criticized me, never demeaned me, never devalued me, and poured his life into me to make me a fishing boat captain. But what about the unreasonable authority figures in my life—the overdemanding boss, the controlling pastor, the authoritarian and demeaning teacher—those who just want to use me or take from me? Even then, God's established principle applies of honoring them and making what is important to them important to me.

This doesn't mean we should submit even to the point of going against the Word of God. The Christians in the Roman Empire refused to go against the Word of God, and many of them were martyred for it. But there is a principle that says if we resist authority, there is an issue in our heart that opposes the ordinance of God and opens the door to fear and judgment in our life.

When we dishonor authority, it is though we are saying, "If God put this authority in my life, then what a poor manager He is!" Whenever we do not have a heart attitude of honor to those in authority, we are dishonoring God. We may think He has given us a raw deal, never realizing that God puts authority in our lives as a minister of good.

Consequently, those who oppose God will "receive condemnation upon themselves." Does God condemn us? No, the Father judges no one (see John 5:22). He doesn't have to judge us; we take pretty good care of opening the door to self-imposed curses; for when we oppose authority, we come into agreement with the first spiritual orphan—the father of lies who is a legalist. When we oppose authority, we come into agreement with the law, and we bring condemnation upon ourselves. God doesn't curse us; rather the enemy has been looking for every open door through which to come in and steal, kill, and destroy. If he can align us with orphan thinking by our agitated resistance against authority, it will give him a key to our front door, and then the enemy has legal ground to come and go in our house as he pleases.

The sonship principle of humility, honor, and submission applies even to unreasonable authority; in Rome's case, it was murderous, immoral, and corrupt authority. When we submit to unreasonable authority, we position ourselves to see God bless, honor, and elevate us in the midst of and in spite of that unreasonable authority. Inheritance is for sons, and God can release inheritance under any circumstances to sons who are subject to Father's mission.

Paul continues in the next few verses:

> *For rulers are not a cause of fear for good behavior, but for evil. Do you want to have no fear of authority? Do what is good and you will have praise from the same; for it is a minister of God to you for good. But if you do what is evil, be afraid; for it does not bear the sword for nothing; for it is a minister of God, an avenger who brings wrath on the one who practices evil. Therefore it is necessary to be in subjection, not only because of*

wrath, but also for conscience' sake. For because of this you also pay taxes, for rulers are servants of God, devoting themselves to this very thing. Render to all what is due them: tax to whom tax is due; custom to whom custom; fear to whom fear; honor to whom honor. Owe nothing to anyone except to love one another; for he who loves his neighbor has fulfilled the law (Romans 13:3-8 NAS).

Why does God want us to submit to unreasonable authority? Following the principle of submitting to all authority helps us learn to respect legitimate authority in spite of their personal blind spots. Every person in authority in our lives has character flaws, and it is easy for us to use those character flaws as justification for rejecting their authority. We need to learn to honor all people, and with our love fulfill the whole law. Submitting to all authority also helps uncover orphan thinking that may remain in us so that we can bring it to the Cross.

Have you forgiven the people who have misrepresented Father's love to you? Why not make a list of those in authority who have hurt you—at work, at school, or in the church. Now, out loud, choose to forgive each one and speak the details of the hurt or disappointment. By forgiving them and letting go of the offense, you will begin to close the door that has been open to condemnation and that has given the enemy the key to traffic in your life.

In the fifth truth toward moving from slavery to sonship, I share my own real-life mistakes and self-imposed curses during my personal quest to discover sonship.

Truth #5. You May Need to Seek Forgiveness From Those in Authority

As with parental authority, simply forgiving earthly or spiritual authority for wounding you may not be enough to break destructive patterns in your life. If you realize that you have caused others pain through weapons of dishonor or brought defilement through ungodly attitudes or behavior, you may find it necessary to go to them for forgiveness and, perhaps, restitution. (See Appendix B for more on the ministry of restitution.)

When I resigned as a Salvation Army Officer in 1986, I left with a good spirit. I had had a bad spirit for two years, but Phillip, a pastor in the area who had begun to mentor me, said, "You can't leave with a bad spirit." So before I resigned, I called headquarters and asked forgiveness from them for my agitated resistance against their policies.

After I left, I went back to the sea, captaining a sport-fishing boat out of Murrell's Inlet, South Carolina, and began attending Pastor Phillip's church, a small Spirit-filled church of about 75 (at that time). I aligned myself to Pastor Phillip, who was like a brother to me and a year older. In addition, our children were the same ages. I positioned myself underneath Pastor Phillip, supporting and helping him in any way I could.

When I left the Salvation Army, the church I had pastored was the fastest-growing church in our division. We were helping the poor and down-and-out, and many people were saved. Now, being aligned with Pastor Phillip, I went to him during my first week there and asked, "Phillip, is there anything I can do? I just want to get underneath; I just want to serve you."

"Yes, there is," he replied. "On the bulletin board, there is a sign-up sheet for those who will commit to cleaning the church and the bathrooms every week. Why don't you sign up?"

I thought, *Don't you know that I was near the top of my class in Bible school and was elected lifetime president? I pastored the fastest-growing church in my district, and you want me cleaning toilets? I've grown beyond that.* But what I actually said was, "Well, I'll think about it." So I got in my car and left, and I thought about it. The

Holy Spirit said to me, "Uh-huh, just look what you're full of." I turned around, went back to the church, and put my wife's name on the list. Later, she made sure I was always right beside her as we cleaned the church together.

I was willing to do anything Pastor Phillip needed. If the usher didn't show up, I ushered. If the nursery worker for Sunday morning didn't show up, I volunteered. I held babies and got puked on. I did anything I could to get underneath Pastor Phillip and push up. And it is funny how quickly you find out what you are full of when doing commode ministry. Toilet ministry offers you some of your greatest opportunities for growth!

Moving Up

After 18 months serving at Pastor Phillip's church, I learned that his father, also a pastor, was looking for a new staff member. Pastor Miles' church had grown to a couple thousand people who were moving into a new sanctuary. A few months earlier, the worship leader had become discontent and walked off with over 100 people. The rift had wounded the soul of the church, and Pastor Miles needed somebody new, somebody who had not been around during the split, to come in and help restore trust.

Pastor Phillip repeatedly said to his father, "Jack has the heart for it. He has a heart of honor, humility, and servanthood. He is even willing to clean toilets. His example will help heal the soul of the church."

In order to feel me out before making a commitment, Pastor Miles asked me to go to Japan and China with him and Phillip for three weeks. He and Pastor Phillip even helped make a way for it to happen financially by scheduling me to speak in meetings so people had an opportunity to sow into my trip.

As we were preparing to return home from China, I could not stop weeping as my heart was moved with compassion for so many broken and impoverished people who didn't know Christ. I felt it was time to leave the sea once more and return to ministry. Pastor Miles approached me saying, "Jack, I want you to move to Spartanburg, South Carolina where I live and help at the church." I acknowledged that I was open to it. He wanted to know what I felt I had to offer the church and what position I should take. My response was, "I believe I need to start on maintenance. I'll serve in the church, but my heart is not mature enough for a staff position." He said he would sleep on it.

The next morning at breakfast, Pastor Miles said, "Jack, because you are willing to start in a low place, I believe your character is mature enough to start as an associate pastor. I want you to be pastor over evangelism and missions. I also need you to help restore trust in the men in the church and to focus your time upon ministering to them." So, we decided that in January 1988, I would go on staff at the largest Spirit-filled church in South Carolina.

Because of the heart of sonship I had toward Pastor Phillip and because I sought to make what was important to him important to me, a staff position at Evangel Cathedral was offered to me rather than to others more educated and experienced. It was my inheritance. I wasn't chosen because of my ability to speak; I was chosen because of my willingness to scrub toilets and a desire in me to make what was important to my authority important to me.

When my family and I finally arrived in Spartanburg, I was so excited! I'd had such a spirit of sonship with Pastor Phillip who was like a brother, and now I was dealing with his father 24 years older than me. Dealing with a brother figure and relating to a father figure were two different things to this spiritual orphan, and I was about to find out what my heart was full of. Remember, I would act like a son as long as someone was making decisions to benefit me. Outwardly, I appeared humble and honoring, but inwardly I unconsciously valued authority for what they could do for me.

For a whole year, I never failed to make what was important to Pastor Miles important to me, and he began entrusting me to fill the pulpit more and more on Sundays when he was out of town. I became one of the congregation's favorite speakers and staff members. Within six months, because of my passionate and aggressive loyalty, Pastor Miles also placed me on the ruling executive board of the church. Decision after decision was made by Pastor Miles that benefited me and helped fulfill my dreams. I was moving up, and my soul reveled in the attention and affirmation!

Orphan Heart Exposed

I was one of nine associate pastors on staff, and early on in my tenure I had moved into sibling rivalry and competition with other staff members for Pastor Miles' attention and speaking opportunities. I was a man of integrity, purity, and of the Spirit, yet I still classically followed the orphan thinking that is found in Chapter Six and on the chart found in Appendix A. There is nothing easier than self-deception, which I never saw coming.

You do not know what you're full of until your boss, pastor, or authority in your life makes a decision that you don't agree with or one that benefits others more than you. A new staff member came on the team who was struggling with orphan issues himself. It was obvious that he was seeking to move his way to the top and become the favored son in Pastor Miles' eyes and the favored staff member to the church. It appeared to me that more and more decisions were being made that benefited him, and I began to receive it as personal offense. Consequently, I closed my heart to Pastor Miles and began the downward spiral along the 12 steps of the spiritual orphan we looked at in Chapter Two. I started noticing

Pastor Miles' faults and weaknesses and could not get my focus off them.

Pastor Miles then began asking, "Jack, is everything all right?" And I would respond as if things were fine. Orphan hearts are usually pretty dysfunctional. They don't trust people enough to talk about their feelings.

I came to work every day doing everything right outwardly, but inwardly I was moving into numb-numb-ville in the sea of fear, snared by my entanglements. I began to think that everyone else was missing God, and I was the only one hearing clearly from Him.

Pastor Miles asked again, "Jack, is everything all right?"

"Yeah, everything is fine." Months went by, and he continued to question me. Our relationship went from very open and transparent to a closed one, because I had shut the door on my end.

Pastor Miles had been in ministry over 40 years. He was a man of honor, integrity, consistency, and great wisdom. He knew that I was no longer being honest and real, but I did not know that he knew it; so, I kept wearing my religious mask and aggressively striving to achieve recognition and favor.

As I felt others were being more favored than me, I also began feeling that he was not being fair with me, so I practiced forgiving him every day, but often forgiveness is not enough. There needs to be open and honest communication and possibly even the walking out of the ministry of restitution. With the loss of trust in me, Pastor Miles rotated me off the executive board, which I received as rejection. The more I closed my heart, the harder I worked, because now I felt that I had to earn my way back into his graces through hyper-religious activity. But the harder I labored, the more deeply into orphan thinking I sank. It began to consume me every waking moment. I no longer valued the unheralded aspects of ministry but hungered to be seen and heard and to have greater authority.

Every Sunday I taught the Equipping Class on Spiritual Authority from Watchman Nee's book of the same title. My life was full of outward loyalty, integrity, purity, service, and faithfulness. I never intentionally spoke against Pastor Miles. I didn't consciously criticize or demean him publicly. I never sought to undermine him. But my heart was closed to him and he could feel it, so trust was lost.

Looking Good!

Feeling like I was on the outside looking in, the father of lies led me unconsciously into self-deception. Because my orphan heart had such a deep need for the approval of man, my words were often directed at influencing people to see how caring, wise, and right I was. I often said things in such a way that put me in a better light in the congregation's eyes than other staff members. People with whom I was in relationship with began to believe that I cared more about them than Pastor Miles did. They began believing that my focus in ministry should be the vision of every church. It really gave me "warm fuzzies" for people to whom I ministered to agree with me and think I was anointed and wise! But it also demonstrated my immaturity and my need for the praise and agreement of man.

Totally unaware of it at that time, I stepped into *marginal deception*. This does not involve a direct lie; rather, it is sharing information or speaking in such a way that influences a person to form conclusions that are beneficial to me. Marginal deception occurs when I give only partial information or relate circumstances in a way that influences people to come into agreement with my point of view.

Due to my unhealed need for love and affirmation that manifested as an orphan heart, I unknowingly was influencing others to form wrong conclusions about the senior pastor to which I never sought to bring correction or proper clarity. This was also done by the absence of *deflected praise*. Deflected praise occurs when someone speaks words of honor or affirmation to me and I, in turn, share the glory with others who are part of the team. When I did not deflect praise, it resulted in my taking illegitimate praise unto myself. It made me look good, but it also drew people's hearts to me and away from Pastor Miles and other associate pastors. It revealed that my heart was insecure with God's affectionate love and that I still struggled with rejection and the need to be needed and affirmed by man.

One of my duties was to visit the hospitals and people's homes each week. Often the people I visited would say something like, "Oh, you have such a caring and pastoral heart! Pastor Miles used to visit, but he doesn't have time for me anymore. But you take time from your busy schedule every week. God bless you!"

I would often respond, "He is very busy, but I will be sure to visit and pray with you, and if you need anything, just call me." I would illegitimately take praise unto myself by not deflecting it back to Pastor Miles. I believed that I was 100-percent loyal to him, when in reality I was unconsciously relishing in drawing the hearts of the people to myself.

Deflected praise would have responded, "As the church began to grow, Pastor Miles started paying me a salary in order to visit you. I am here only because he has sent me to you. I am personally representing him and know that he is praying for you. Next time you see him, thank him for sending me to visit you."

Can you see how easy it is for orphan hearts to be deceived by what seems right and fair to them? We need to be independent of needing something from someone before we can effectively lead them or minister to their needs. Otherwise, we unconsciously become manipulative in our pursuit for affirmation, acceptance, and achievement. We are often left with a sense of heaviness or guilt and feel insecure in our relationships. This binds others to us in an unhealthy, codependent relationship, because we want them to need and admire us and to think that we are more mature and wiser than we really are.

These two areas (marginal deception and deflected praise) in which I struggled revealed how deeply the orphan heart had deceived me. I was subject to my own mission and was illegitimately winning hearts, and I never saw it. Even though I had integrity and thought that I was being totally loyal, it was such an easy thing to unknowingly draw people's hearts to myself. This held me back from maturity, promotion, and favor with God and man. In the church, I unconsciously caused tension and division in the spiritual realm because of my lack of maturity and my need to feel accepted and liked.

Leveling Off

Over the next year and a half, I experienced some of the worst emotional pain and confusion that I had known since my childhood when I felt that I did not have a place in my father's heart. During this same season, I was being trained in every type of deliverance and prayer counseling ministry. I was leading prayer counseling sessions with men and started ministering to pastors and their families. I could set others free but was becoming more and more personally bound by orphan thinking.

Over that year and a half, there was a lot of betrayal and hurt from another staff member who brought division to the staff as he tried to win Pastor Miles' heart by making other staff members' motives seem questionable. Something inside me needed Pastor Miles to put me back into a high-profile place before the people. It was my orphan heart, always striving but never achieving, always longing but never satisfied.

People would come up to me and say, "You're my favorite speaker on staff; why don't you speak much anymore?" It was like getting kicked in the gut to have to say, "Well, Pastor Miles just wants to give others an opportunity," while inwardly I was seething with hurt and disappointment. And of course, I felt that I didn't have a problem; it was all Pastor Miles' fault! I thought he was unjust and unfair, because as an orphan I could not recognize my own closed spirit. Every time Pastor Miles came around, I would run to him with my "IV system," telling him all the wonderful things I was doing, hoping he would pat me on the back and tell me how wonderful I was. Do you see what kind of craziness an orphan spirit will drive you to?

I started turning in reports on all the ministry I was accomplishing so he would know how hard I was slaving for him in the church. After all, an orphan is a slave, not a son. During this time, I felt that I was a man of absolute integrity, truth, and character, and I slaved away 70 hours a week. I was one of the favorite pastoral care persons on staff, but I'd lost trust in Pastor Miles' eyes because I lacked an open heart and wasn't honest with him, and he could feel it. Every time he asked how I was doing, I continued to assure him that everything was fine. No problems. But I wasn't real, and I didn't know he could see through my religious mask as easily as he did.

Things at the church for me just slowly leveled out, but we never talked through this issue. I wanted to resign many times, but my mentor, Pastor Phillip, would not agree to me leaving. He told me, "You do not leave when you feel that the chips are down, or you will repeat the pattern in the next place you go. You leave only when you are sent out blessed."

Finally, things balanced out. The other staff member fueling dissension was exposed. I received some restoration of recognition and authority, and then I felt released to leave. I went to Pastor Miles and said, "You know, I'm getting so caught up in prayer ministry to leaders and pastors that I really feel like this is what I'm to do with my life."

He said, "I agree; that's where your anointing lies, and that is what you need to do. I'll bless you and send you out. I'll give you three months' pay to get the ministry off the ground, and I'll even take up an offering for you." Despite my orphan heart, he did everything he could to bless me. Pastor Miles is known to be a man of impeccable character who is generous and full of grace. He has never had a moral or ethical compromise in his life or ministry.

Moving Out

So we started Shiloh Place Ministries in January 1991 and lived in poverty for the next seven years. We had a particular anointing for prayer counseling ministry, so I went into churches and conducted prayer counseling seminars. Pastor Miles was now Bishop Miles, and overseer of a growing ministers' fellowship—Evangel Fellowship International (EFI), of which I was a part. Twice a year I attended the pastors' meeting with Bishop Miles, but in all those times we were together he never promoted my ministry as he did others. He never invited me to speak at one of their conferences.

I was sitting there with too few meeting engagements, too little money, barely able to feed my family, and inside I was seething because he was promoting others and not me. My orphan thinking went something like this: *I've got more integrity than they do. I've not had a moral failure like some have. And besides, I'm the guy who's been helping many of these folks' marriages!* I was on my own mission and was mad because I felt nobody was underneath pushing me up.

I had an effective ministry. God had used my wife and me to help save many marriages, but Bishop Miles wouldn't promote me. All he had to do was bring me up on that platform one time in front of the ministers' fellowship and say, "Jack Frost has an incredible ministry; you need to get him in your church," and financial prosperity would have come to us practically overnight. But he never did it. He did it with those, who in my eyes, had less integrity than me, but he wouldn't do it with me. No sonship, no inheritance! No sonship, no influence!

In my weakest hour, when orphan thinking threatened to sink my boat, God's love found me. In November 1995, I received a deep personal revelation of Father's love that transformed my life as much as when I received Christ. Trisha said, "Jack was transformed more in 45 minutes in Father's embrace than he was the previous 15 years combined as a Christian." (Read about this in my first book, *Experiencing Father's Embrace*.) The anointing on my life and ministry increased greatly. Yet, I still had never talked over the issues with Pastor Miles regarding the time I was on staff with him.

I had let seven years pass with no closure—seven years of the enemy having a key to my front door. Then in October 1997, I went to a church pastored by a friend of mine named Roger to conduct an Experiencing Father's Embrace Encounter. Roger was one of the ruling elders and closest friends of Pastor Miles and had been a mentor to me since the mid-1980s. After driving me and my team to the motel and dropping the others off to go inside, Roger asked me to stay behind. When we were alone in the car, he said to me, "Jack, do you realize that EFI elders and Pastor Miles do not have faith and trust in your ministry?"

I had suspected it for a long time but never had any facts, just an undercurrent of feeling. I went through the roof in anger and frustration at the situation of sometimes being unable to buy clothes for the kids or keep enough food on the table when all the time it was within the power of others to promote me and bless me.

And all this time I was so sure it was their fault when in reality it was mine. I had brought it all on myself. Remember Hebrews 13:17: *"Obey your leaders and submit to them, for they keep watch over your souls as those who will give an account. Let them do this with joy and not with grief, for this would be unprofitable for you*" (NAS). Could Bishop Miles look at me with joy, or did he look at me with grief? Because my orphan heart hindered me from being open, honest, and real, he could look at me only with grief, which was unprofitable for me. As Romans 13:2 warns, I had brought condemnation upon myself—a self-imposed curse that became an open door for the enemy to traffic through.

But sitting in the car with Roger that day, I just couldn't see that I was at fault. Instead, I wanted to justify, blame-shift, and make myself look innocent. Roger said, "They feel like you just relate to EFI and the pastors for what they can do for you. You have never yet sought to be honest with Pastor Miles and resolve your issues with him from when you were on staff."

I went home after those meetings angry and called my friend and brother, Pastor Phillip. I asked him, "Phillip, are you aware that your dad and the elders of EFI do not have trust in my ministry?"

"Yes, I am, Jack."

"You and I are in covenant together. Why haven't you told me before?"

"Because I didn't think you were mature enough to handle it, and your angry attitude is revealing that you apparently are not."

I was so mad I was ready to leave the ministry—again. I was ready to leave the ministers' fellowship. I was ready to walk away from relationships I'd had for years and go back to deep-sea fishing. "Gales and 20-foot seas are easier to deal with than people!"

Seeing the Light

I honestly could not see what I had been doing wrong. So, I did what I had learned to do in times of crisis—I went into solitude for several days to pray and fast. About the fourth day, I felt the Holy Spirit prompt me to write down every way that I had valued people and the church for what they could do for me. I wrote down the emotions and attitudes that I had struggled with for ten years. One thing about fasting—three or four days into it and you'll find out what you're full of! I saw it. And it was one of the ugliest things I have ever seen! I had typed nine, single-spaced pages of self-centered, self-consuming, and self-referential behavior. I realized that my relationships were built upon what others could do for me and that I had been subject to my own mission all these years. I defiled the church and EFI because I was not there to get underneath and push up Bishop Mile's vision, only my own.

When you pray two hours a day, read ten chapters of the Bible a day, fast 50-60 days a year, go into regular five-day solitude retreats alone with God; when you've never gone back to pornography, when you've never had an integrity failure, when you're doing all the right things and people still don't trust or promote you, then obviously it must be their fault, because look how righteous you are. It sickened me to see all the pride and self-righteousness and self-justification that filled my heart. I was the chief of all spiritual orphans.

When I finally saw the ugliness of my orphan heart, I immediately went to my mentor and said, "Phillip, please forgive me; I see now what you're saying." Then I called Roger, explained my revelation, and asked, "What do I need to do?" I realized that it was not enough just to forgive and to be forgiven; I needed to go to those I had misrepresented God's love to and make restitution.

Making Restitution

I was terrified at the thought of approaching Bishop Miles because my orphan heart was intimidated by authority. I had such a fear of man. It was pure orphan thinking. So, because Roger lived nearby, I asked him to go with me. He said, "I'll meet you there and walk with you through this."

I had sent a copy of my nine-page confession to Bishop Miles in advance so he could read it before we met. As we sat down at lunch together, we chatted, and he was as friendly as could be. That helped set me more at ease. I said to Bishop Miles, "You received the letter that I sent you?"

"Yes, I did."

"Did you read it?"

"Every word."

"Bishop Miles," I said, "I want to ask you to forgive me for all these years that I valued you for what you could do for me." I also confessed to him that I had put a demand on our relationship—I wanted him to be my source of affirmation and promotion, and not God. It resulted in me operating in control and manipulation, trying to get my unhealed need met. Furthermore, I confessed the defilement I had brought into his church and all the people I drew to myself who had gotten underneath me instead of deflecting praise to him.

He said, "Jack, I forgave you back in 1989. I tried to talk to you about it, but every time I tried, you insisted everything was fine. I lost trust in you because you weren't honest with me."

And we wonder why promotion doesn't seem to come our way in the workplace or in our church. Promotion is often delayed for orphans; or it is illegitimately taken at a high price to our relationships, character, and integrity. Orphans feel the need to fight and wrangle for everything they want. That's probably one reason why there is so much strife and division in our churches. Spiritual orphans are competing with each other for position, any morsel of affirmation, or the praise of man.

We wonder why much of the church is powerless in our nations and our cities, and why many flock to other religions or cults. Could it be because of so many orphan hearts that misrepresent Father's love to their families and to the world?

Bishop Miles forgave me, blessed me, and sent me on my way with these words, "Jack, you have really matured. I do not know many men who would have humbled themselves the way you have. I am proud of you, and I believe in you. God is about to do something great through your life!"

God told me in 1980 that I would take healing and restoration to the nations of the earth. Later, Bill Hamon and five or six other prophets confirmed it prophetically. For 17 years, I had slaved to make that word come to pass, but it never did. I worked, I labored, I did everything to build the ministry, and yet few people in authority would get behind me. Few would promote me, even though I helped thousands of people. I struggled, had no money, and little backing. It was not until I confessed and renounced my orphan heart, made restitution to the authorities I had defied and defiled, and embraced the spirit of sonship that the prophecy began to be fulfilled. No sonship, no influence. No sonship, no inheritance.

There may be a need for you to go to pastoral or other authority and make restitution to them for being an orphan toward them instead of a son. Don't do it because I did it; do it because the Holy Spirit convicts you to do so. Take a few minutes to sit quietly and ask God to show you any persons in authority who you may need to go to and make things right. It may be a past or present boss, pastor, or teacher. Write their names down. Then read the "Ministry of Restitution" in Appendix B at the end of this book. It will explain how to begin to move toward bringing closure in your relationships. As you do, you will also progress in your journey from slavery to sonship.

CHAPTER TEN

JACK'S BANK

Jack's Bank was the name that a few fishermen gave to one of the hottest grouper fishing spots ever found off the Outer Banks of North Carolina. They named it that, because every time I hit this super secret spot, I was heading to the bank when I got home. In the winter of 1982, I caught 75,000 pounds of snowy grouper on hook-and-line on one shipwreck in a two-month period. It was over $80,000 in fish sales, and my captain's pay alone after all expenses, was over $25,000. Not bad for two months of the most adventurous fishing I have ever known.

It was January 1982, and I had received Christ as my Savior only two years earlier. I felt that God was speaking to me to leave my life as a commercial fishing captain and go to Bible school in order to lay a foundation for giving the rest of my life to taking a message of healing and restoration to the nations. I was very insecure with that idea because my whole identity had been wrapped up in being Top Hook, one of the best snapper and grouper fishermen on the southeast coast. Bible school and ministry had too many intimidating uncertainties. So I bargained with God, "If in the next few months, You pay off all my debts and provide the money my wife and I need for us both to attend two years of Bible school, I will receive that as confirmation that I need to step out of my comfort zone and into faith." I was willing, but I thought I found a way out of leaving the sea and obeying God.

The very next commercial fishing trip following that deal, I found myself 28 miles off Ocracoke, North Carolina, fishing for red snapper in 240 feet of water on the continental shelf. We fished all night and boated about a thousand pounds, and then headed east to the 100 fathom curve (600 feet deep) to fish for deep-water snowy grouper during the day hours. As we motored to the east, I put the boat on auto-pilot while my two crewmen were sleeping in their bunks. It should have been only a one-hour run, but I fell asleep at the wheel and went several miles farther east than where I had been before. When I awoke and looked at my fish-finding scope, I saw the largest school of grouper that I had ever seen sitting on top of a wreck in 840 feet of water.

As we anchored on this previously undiscovered and uncharted wreck, we caught 9,000 pounds of snowy grouper within the next 30 hours. Every fish weighed between 50 and 60 pounds. It took a day to return to the dock and another day to unload and sell those fish. We turned the boat around and went right back and caught another 9,000 pounds in less than another 30 hours. I made $7,400 captain's share in just six days.

It was my inheritance. I was willing (though skeptical) to give up everything that had made me secure in life—my identity at sea—and be obedient to the word that I felt God had given me to leave the sea and follow Him. I was so thankful that God had set me free from drug and porn addiction that I just wanted to be subject to God's mission in life and not my own. But it would take supernatural intervention financially to build my faith to leave my mistress, the sea.

During winter time, it is very difficult to find two or three consecutive days of weather calm enough to fish deep water off the Outer Banks. These treacherous waters are known as the

Graveyard of the Atlantic because of the many ships that have gone down there. So, over the next two months, there were very few days that I could fish Jack's Bank, and to complicate matters, every fishing boat in the fleet wanted to catch me on this "bonanza" where Captain Jack, on his boat, *The Life of a King*, was catching more fish in a day than most boats caught in a month.

It is difficult to put into words the passion and faith that I found in God during this season of reaping the harvest that He had prepared for me. I knew beyond a shadow of a doubt that the discovery of Jack's Bank was a supernatural God thing and that He was providing everything I needed to transition my life of being so entangled in the world system to a life given over to seeking the Kingdom of God and making it known to the world.

For two months, the fleet tried to catch me on Jack's Bank in order to steal my inheritance. When at port, I would keep my boat fully equipped with fuel, bait, ice, fishing gear, and food, and wait until a winter storm passed through. Then on the last day of a freezing gale, at 2 o'clock in the morning, I would sneak *The Life of a King* (a 44-foot Thompson) away from the dock while all others were in their warm and cozy beds. When the other captains came to the dock at Morehead City, North Carolina (my home port at this time) the next day, they would see my boat gone and had no idea the direction I took. By the time the weather was nice enough for others to go out, I would have beaten my way through 8- to 12-foot seas and be ready to fish as soon as the sea would die down. Then within 24 hours, I would have my boat loaded with snowy grouper and be on my way home while the rest of the fleet was on their way out. I must say that I wasn't driven only by the calling of God on my life, but also by a boatload of pride and ego at slyly outsmarting the fleet. Even now, 25 years later, my emotions can feel the glory of those weeks.

Finally, the captain of a boat named the *Blue Water* wised up. He too had his boat outfitted and ready to go, and started sleeping on the boat, waiting to hear my Detroit diesel engine fire up in the middle of the night. With the help of darkness, rough seas, and radar (I had no radar), he followed me to the northeast from a safe distance in the middle of the night and all through the next day. As the winds calmed down, I anchored up on Jack's Bank and started pulling grouper two at a time, when the *Blue Water* snuck up off my bow and caught me on the fish. The problem was that he had no idea that Jack's Bank was in 840 feet of water, and he didn't have enough anchor line to fish this depth. He caught a few fish drifting, but the current was too strong to drift-fish. I outfished him 6,600 pounds to his 600 for those few days at sea before a severe winter storm drove us home.

Whether he was jealous, or ashamed that I had outfished him, or just wanted revenge for "putting it to him" so badly, I'm not sure—but the *Blue Water* revealed the location of the shipwreck to the rest of the fleet, and they in turn went out and burned out (caught all the fish) Jack's Bank. Under the cover of darkness, they were able to steal the rest of my inheritance that I believe God had laid up for me. The $25,000 I made from Jack's Bank did help prepare Trisha and me for the next two years of Bible school, but there could have been thousands more if I had been a little wiser to the schemes of others who sought to plunder my inheritance.

So many Christians have received Christ and have the right to be joint heirs with Him. Everything we see in Christ we are an heir too, but sometimes jealousy, shame, or feeling that others are more blessed seem to hold us back. At other times, it just seems that the thief steals the blessings of God right out from under us. Whatever it may be, many people do not receive their inheritance because of two important truths that were robbing me for years of provision and fruitfulness in my life and family. Let's see how much they may be hindering you from being subject to Father's mission.

An orphan heart is bound up and steeped in lies and ungodly beliefs that have their source in the father of lies. Consequently, an orphan does not legitimately receive an inheritance. Orphans live in the realm of untruth and darkness while inheritance belongs to the realm of truth and light.

This contrast between truth and lies leads us to the sixth truth in our quest to move from slavery to sonship.

Truth #6. Daily Renounce Ungodly Beliefs and Hidden Lies of Orphan Thinking.

Proverbs 23:7 says that we become according to what we think in our hearts. If you think like an orphan, you will live like an orphan. If you think you do not have a home, you will live life as if you don't have a home. If you think like a son, you will live like a son. If you think you have a home, you will live life as if you have a home. A key truth to displacing orphan thinking is to expose the lies and ungodly beliefs that are at its core and let light dispel the darkness. It is a daily battle that we all fight. In fact, Paul describes it in blatantly warlike terms:

> *For the weapons of our warfare are not of the flesh, but divinely powerful for the destruction of fortresses. We are destroying speculations and every lofty thing raised up against the knowledge of God, and we are taking every thought captive to the obedience of Christ* (2 Corinthians 10:4-5 NAS).

The word *speculations* in Greek means, "reasonings, thoughts, and imaginations that precede and determine our conduct." "Fortresses" or strongholds in themselves are not demonic; this Scripture refers to a fortress of thought that includes lies against what God has revealed about Himself. It is a habit structure of thinking that exalts itself above the knowledge of God's love. The fortress of thought gives the enemy ground to traffic in your life. If you cast out the demonic influence but let the fortress of thought remain, then the demonic influence has a legal right to return and to reoccupy the fortress.

Our minds are either influenced by the Father of Creation or the father of lies. We saw in Chapter Two the 12-step downward spiral that orphan thinking takes that culminates in a stronghold of oppression. Only in daily walking in the truth of Christ can such a stronghold be displaced. One of the biggest dangers in all of this is the fact that so often lies and ungodly beliefs creep into our thoughts so subtly that we don't recognize them as orphan thinking.

In January 1998, a couple of months after my act of confession and restitution (see Chapter Nine) with Bishop Miles, Trisha said to me, "I had a dream last night about your upcoming trip to Poland." I was scheduled to attend a pastors' conference in northern Poland during May of that year. Trisha continued, "I dreamed that Bishop Miles was with you. Why don't you call him and invite him to go with you?"

"He doesn't have time for me," I replied. Did you catch that? Do you see how orphan thinking twists our thought life? True, Bishop Miles was a very busy man who regularly traveled internationally. His time was precious, and I immediately assumed that I had no value to him and he could spare none of his time for me. So I left it alone.

The next day Trisha said, "I had that dream again. You really need to call Bishop Miles."

"He's booked years in advance," I protested, "He's not going to take time for me." Again I was thinking like I was a little bitty nothing, an orphan nobody values or would promote. Nobody was going to favor me; nobody cared about me. Do you see how quickly and easily we can come into agreement with the accuser of the brethren—the first spiritual orphan?

For the next few nights, Trisha had the same dream about Bishop Miles being with me in Poland. She took the risk of being a nag and kept insisting that I call him.

Finally, I picked up the phone and called his office, believing I would not get through to him. I spoke to his secretary, "I'd like to schedule a phone appointment with Bishop Miles for any time he is available."

She put her hand over the phone, and I heard her say, "Bishop Miles, this is Jack Frost; he'd like to get with you."

"I'd love to talk to him right now," he replied.

There went one ungodly belief blown right out the door! I couldn't believe he was there and available and sounding genuinely interested in talking to me.

Bishop Miles got on the phone. "Hello, Jack. How are you doing?"

"Things are going pretty well," I said. "In fact, they're going great."

"So, tell me about what God is doing."

"Well, we have a pastors' conference in Poland coming up in May, and I was wondering if you would come with me and be one of the key speakers."

"I can't believe you're calling me," he replied with excitement in his voice. "Two years ago, I felt that God told me to go to Poland. I don't know anybody there, and I've been praying ever since for an open door to Poland. I'll adjust my schedule and come with you."

And just like that, Bishop Miles went to Poland with me. He flew into Warsaw on one airline, and I flew in on another. He met me at the gate, having arrived an hour ahead of me. As we walked out to the baggage claim, this man who had been faithful in ministry for over 40 years, and whom I had served under for three, put his hand on my shoulder and said, "Now, Jack, I'm here to serve you."

"But Bishop Miles," I protested, "you're the apostle. You're the one who…"

"This is your conference, Jack. You're the host and you invited me. I don't even need to speak. I just want to be here to help you with anything you need."

And I'm thinking, *And my orphan heart had trouble receiving this humble man's servant heart all these years?*

Breakthrough

So we went to the conference, and I opened up teaching on Father's transforming love. The central European pastors were weeping in travail as Bishop Miles sat there watching in amazement. By the fourth day, most of the 90 pastors present were on their faces on the floor in repentance. Many went to their wives and asked forgiveness for sinning against love. Having observed and absorbed this all week, Bishop Miles asked, "How soon can you come back to Evangel Cathedral and conduct an Experiencing Father's Embrace Encounter? How soon can you come to the ministers' fellowship and teach this to all the ministers?"

Since I had left Bishop Miles' church in 1991, he had never invited me back to speak. His church was huge, and I was used to ministering in churches of 50 to 100 people where the offerings often would be barely enough to cover my travel expenses.

I replied, "My calendar is pretty clear. I can come whenever you want."

"How soon can you go to Russia with me and teach our 300 pastors there on the Father's love?"

"Whenever you want."

"As soon as we get home, I'm going to call all the elders of the ministers' fellowship and tell them that they need to get this revelation in their church."

Bishop Miles was true to his word. When he returned, he started calling pastors he knew, and almost overnight our little impoverished ministry that was used to barely getting by began receiving all kinds of invitations from larger churches.

When I came to Bishop Miles' church for the Encounter and stepped into the pulpit that Sunday morning, I knew I couldn't speak until I cleansed the defilement I had released upon the church that I spoke about in the previous chapter. Standing before those 1,500 people I said, "Before I can ever speak in this pulpit, I have to ask this church to forgive me because I unconsciously defiled the soul of this church when I was on staff here for three years in the late 1980s. I was not here to serve this pastor; I was here to serve myself, and I used many of you to try and meet my need to be needed. I ask every person here to forgive me for trying to use you and Bishop Miles to promote my life and ministry. Please forgive me."

All over the building people broke down weeping. Talk about a powerful conference!

Not long after this, I went to the ministers' fellowship meeting. Bishop Miles asked me to speak on the first night, which was always a night of honor at the fellowship. He introduced me to the 275 pastors who were there and told them that what I had to say was one of the most needed revelations of our day, a vital word for the endtimes. This was the same place where for years I could hardly get a speaking slot or promotion to save my life! But back then, I was an untrustworthy orphan, and now I was moving toward sonship. I had begun walking the path of humility, getting my eyes off others' faults and weaknesses, and acknowledging and confronting orphan thinking and ungodly beliefs inside me that fueled an orphan heart. When we are willing to humble ourselves before God and man, God honors and exalts us in due season.

I stood before those 275 ministers and confessed, "I joined this fellowship in 1986 in its second year when there were only 18 of us. Now there are hundreds, and for the last 12 years, I have done everything I could to promote myself and to manipulate you to further my ministry. I came to meetings with a calendar in hand, hoping I would get a meeting from you. I have related to this fellowship based upon what you could do for me rather than on how I could get underneath and be a blessing to Bishop Miles and to Evangel Fellowship. In my immaturity, I tried to use you. Please forgive me." Needless to say, everyone was shocked because you do not normally hear stuff like that in a ministers' meeting.

Then I shared my testimony of receiving an experiential revelation of Father's love. When the altar ministry began, many of the very same elders who had no trust in my life or ministry before were the first ones at the altar weeping. In fact, some ended up in my arms as we wept together and they asked forgiveness for judging me harshly. Later several pastors from large churches asked, "How soon can you come to my church and teach on Father's love?"

If I had not cast down the ungodly beliefs and invited Bishop Miles to come to Poland with me, the reconciliation of relationships, restoration of trust, and promotion to areas of greater influence might never have happened. Casting down orphan thinking is a daily battle. Acknowledging and renouncing the ungodly beliefs and hidden lies are so important to displacing an orphan heart with the truth of God's transforming love.

In order to help you be more sensitive to whose voice you are listening to, several times a week review the Orphan/Son Contrast chart in Appendix A. The voice of the Father of Creation leads you home into a place of forgiveness, affirmation, love, and rest. The voice of the father of lies leads you away from home into fears, performing for self-worth, self-assertion, self-judgment, self-condemnation, self-consuming, self-promotion, blame-shifting, fault-finding, justifying, and striving to prove yourself innocent in a matter.

Truth #7. Begin Sowing Into Your Inheritance.

As this revelation of orphans and sons became real to me, I discovered another important truth in displacing orphan thinking when I realized that it was time to begin to sow into my inheritance. Prior to this, each December we would get a letter from Evangel Fellowship International (EFI), the fellowship of churches I was a part of, that invited us to participate in receiving a Christmas offering for Bishop Miles. I knew what his salary was, and how often he spoke at other churches, which collected nice offerings for him. And here I was trying to raise a family of five on less than $30,000. "Why didn't they take up an offering for me?" Definitely orphan thinking.

In those days, I did not have the revelation of giving honor to whom honor is due, thus I lacked a heart of sonship. God began to reveal to me how I was dishonoring authority with orphan thinking whenever I felt that authority didn't need a blessing they were receiving as much as I did. It revealed that I had no honor toward authority, thus no sonship.

Sons recognize the power of sowing into their inheritance by seeking to bless those who have blessed them as well as blessing others as they have been blessed. As Paul told the Romans, "*If the Gentiles have shared in their spiritual things, they are indebted to minister to them also in material things*" (Rom. 15:27b NAS). As I encountered this verse in my new mind-set of a son, I realized that I had a debt to all the people who had put up with me in my "teenage" years, my years of spiritual immaturity when I did more taking from people than giving. How much grief and pain had I caused Bishop Miles and some of the other people in my life because of my immaturity in valuing them for what they could do for me and in trying to manipulate them to promote my life and ministry?

Who Are You Indebted To?

The Lord yoked other verses to the one above: "*If we sowed spiritual things in you, is it too much if we reap material things from you?*" (1 Cor. 9:11 NAS). The sixth chapter of Galatians contains a verse that is often taken out of context in Scripture:

> *The one who is taught the word is to share all good things with the one who teaches him. Do not be deceived, God is not mocked; for whatever a man sows, this he will also reap. For the one who sows to his own flesh will from the flesh reap corruption, but the one who sows to the Spirit will from the Spirit reap eternal life* (Galatians 6:6-8 NAS).

Think about all the people you owe a spiritual debt to. Who nurtured you in the faith? Who mentored you? Who matured you in the things of God? Who modeled Father's love for you sincerely, regardless of how imperfectly? Who tolerated being valued by you for what they could do for you rather than for relationship's sake? Have you sowed materially into their lives and ministries? Are you making what is important to them important to you?

When orphan thinking dominated my thought life, every time it came to blessing Bishop Miles or other authorities in any way, I'd cop an attitude. As God opened my eyes to see this, I realized that I'd never repaid my debt. "*Do not be deceived, God is not mocked; for whatever a man sows* [into his spiritual authorities materially], *this he will also reap.*" When a special offering is received for someone in authority in your life and you grieve over it and send the least you can get away with, this verse implies that you will reap nothing but corruption. It can reveal a heart issue of dishonor. No inheritance for orphans. But if you sow to the Spirit, you will reap eternal life. Inheritance is for sons.

Sowing Honor

I began to realize that receiving an offering for Bishop Miles and sowing into his life and ministry was not about meeting his need but about revealing my own heart issues and what I wanted to reap in the future from those who give oversight and account for my life. God really grabbed hold of my heart with this. I sat down with my wife and I showed her the whole thing. "Trisha, we've never joyfully blessed those in authority who put up with us in our years of immaturity. And look how much we have struggled." We gave to the poor, we gave to missions, we give here and there; but because we felt our authority didn't need it or deserve it, we failed to honor them. But it wasn't about their need; it was about whether we were orphans or sons, about whether we were willing to get underneath and push up. It was about our need to sow honor in order that, later in life, we might reap honor and become an influencer for the Kingdom of God in the lives of others.

I told Trisha, "I want us to start giving to the people who have put up with us all through the years and helped us mature." Together we made a list of about five people and began praying for seed to sow: "Father, we don't have any money. We don't have any way to bless these folks. So, Father, in accordance with Romans 15:27, First Corinthians 9:11, and Galatians 6:6-8, we ask You to supply seed for the sower, bread for food, that You might multiply a harvest. Bring increase that we will be prosperous in everything for liberality." We started claiming this daily, and financial increase began to occur.

It began slowly and grew from there. If we received $20 from some unexpected source, we gave $10 to our pastor; $50, we gave him $20. Sometimes I would take the missions offering collected at one of our Encounters and send a portion to Bishop Miles for his upcoming mission trip.

We decided to not make sowing into our inheritance just about finances. It is also about our time, focus, and loyalty. We looked for other ways to bless Bishop Miles and Pastor Phillip. Whatever was important to them, we were going to make important to us and all our team at Shiloh Place Ministries. We searched out every possible way to honor, bless, support, and promote their families, work, and ministry.

When Trisha and I received this revelation about sowing into our inheritance, our income at Shiloh Place Ministries went up 78 percent in the first year. The second year it went up 76 percent. In 1999 and 2000, it went up another 74 percent. After 9-11, many ministries' finances began to decline all over the world, yet ours continued to climb. Everywhere we go, we are astounded at the honor and finances that people entrust us with.

Our tithe belongs at our local church, but beyond that, we continue to sow materially into the people who have ministered to us. It is a biblical principle. We have a debt, and it is an honor to discharge that debt by blessing materially and with our loyalty and emotional support, each of those who have put up with us when we had orphan hearts. That is sowing into our inheritance, and it is helping to displace orphan thinking with a heart of sonship!

Truth #8. Entering Into Your Inheritance.

On our quest for movement from slavery to sonship, the final truth that I have to impart to you is the transformation that I have seen in my life, family, relationships, and ministry. That is the evidence that makes everything written in this book real and something worth pursuing more deeply. Nothing motivates like results!

Over a period of about three years, from 1997 to 1999, the previous seven truths worked through my mind and emotions until they began to become revelation in my spirit. During this time, Trisha and I saw supernatural transformation beginning to take place in many arenas of life. But now, in 2006, it is so very clear to see the inheritance and lasting fruitfulness we stepped into through our quest for rest. Following is listed some of the lasting fruit that has sprung forth from sonship being worked through our heart.

First, I began to discover God's rest. For most of my life, I struggled with the inability to rest and enjoy life. Something always seemed to grip me and pull me into restlessness. Some words to describe how I felt inside were tension, agitation, striving, or stressed. Let's try to give definition to this restlessness—the feeling that there is something more that I have to do or put in order to feel valued, affirmed, accepted, or loved.

Our competitive culture tends to define *rest* as a place of idleness or being unproductive. But the biblical rest found in sonship is not a place without activity or fruitfulness. Rest is a posture of the heart of sonship that feels so sheltered in Father's love that it does not allow itself to be pulled into a place where we strive to feel valued, affirmed, or secure. Abiding in rest is the place where all people will be drawn to us because everyone is searching for rest.

Second, feeling more secure and at rest in Father's love displaced much of my fear—fear of authority, fear of trusting, fear of rejection, and fear of intimacy. When around those in authority or even in a group of people, I no longer feel like I am on the outside looking in and wondering what I have to do to get on the inside. Perfect love has displaced so much of the insecurity and fear of being hurt again.

Third, with fear displaced, our relationships have become much more open, real, and meaningful, and are becoming the community of love that Christ intended for them to be. We are surrounded by true friends who are there for us, no matter what, and we seek to be there for them. We have seen the yoke of independence broken and embraced interdependent friendships.

Fourth, I helped my mom and dad receive the Lord, and I experienced closure when they passed away. My father died a few years ago, and my mother last year. There is much to say of seeing them pass on to be with the Lord, and your heart feeling innocent of the sins that they committed against you and the dishonor you committed against them. Forgiveness and restitution prevents the accuser of the brethren from binding you with a guilt or victim mentality.

Fifth, the hearts of my children have been restored to my heart. When my heart was full of orphan thinking toward my parents and spiritual authorities, I reaped from my children the same attitudes and relationship. All three of my children are now seeking to walk in a spirit of sonship with me. Can you image the joy and fulfillment that I, as a father, feel in that?

Sixth, all three of my children and the spouses of the two married ones are walking with God and seeking to make His love known to the world. In my orphan years, my children went through their years of rebellion and being seduced by the world. They all have come home to God's love, motivated by the transformation they have seen in their mom and dad.

Seventh, over the last eight years we have seen great favor, honor, and promotion released upon our lives and ministry. Following the act of confession and restitution with Bishop Miles, we have steadily matured into primary influencers in Evangel Fellowship International. We have been made elders in the fellowship and are regular speakers in their ministers' meetings. Outside of EFI, we are looked to as respected apostolic leaders in the nations for the revelation of God as a loving, affectionate, affirming Father.

Eighth, financial provision and increase have been supernatural over the last eight years both in our ministry and personal lives. After 15 years of poverty, the heart of sonship has made a way for us to give hilariously and to be a financial blessing to our children's and grandchildren's future.

Ninth, as we began to focus our life upon being a son and daughter to those in authority in our lives, many of our staff and team members began to do likewise with us and Shiloh Place. As promotion came to us, promotion began to occur in them, and we now have over 70 ministry team members who are traveling the world with the message of God's transforming love and deeply impacting families, churches, and ministers.

Tenth, in eight years we went from a little impoverished, nobody-has-heard-of-us ministry, to an international ministry that is touching the world through our schools, encounters, and resource materials. Many people are coming to know Christ, and many more are having families transformed and hearts healed.

All ten of these things have occurred without self-assertion and aggressive striving to try and make them happen. We settled into God's rest, focused our life upon being a son and daughter, and His love has produced the inheritance. Intimacy preceded fruitfulness. Sonship preceded inheritance and the fulfillment of the word that God gave in 1980—"Leave your identity at sea, and you shall take healing and restoration to the nations."

CONCLUSION

A s long as I tried to build my identity and ministry through orphan thinking, I felt like the angry older brother slaving in the fields and thought that the father had never given me anything to be merry (see Luke 15:25-30). I saw little lasting fruit and was left in a state of agitated resistance against authority and in disappointment and frustration. But as I began to sow into my inheritance by getting underneath and blessing others and earnestly seeking to be faithful with that which was another's, I began to receive the promises of God for my life, family, and ministry.

Have you wondered why you have not seen more lasting fruit in your life? Do you wonder why you don't have more influence in your workplace? Do you wonder why you haven't come into the place that God has called you to in your local church and that you know He wants you to move into? Are you sowing into your inheritance? Or do you cop an attitude when it's time to take up an offering or to bless your pastor or boss at Christmastime?

> *He who is faithful in a very little thing is faithful also in much; and he who is unrighteous in a very little thing is unrighteous also in much....And if you have not been faithful in the use*

of that which is another's, who will give you that which is your own? (Luke 16:10,12 NAS).

Your inheritance, the word God has given you, is delayed until you learn obedience from the things that you suffer by becoming a son or a daughter. Then you begin to become a representative of God's transforming love to your family and others. It is all wrapped up in the principles of honor and submission, of humbling yourself to become faithful with that which is another's, of getting underneath and pushing up, of serving unselfishly and wholeheartedly to build up another with no personal agenda or ulterior motives.

As always, Christ is our example, who said that He *"did not come to be served, but to serve, and to give His life as a ransom for many"* (Matt. 20:28). God opposes the proud. He is not opposed to you, but He is opposed to anything of the orphan heart in you that tries to exalt itself or promote itself.

It's time for sons and daughters to come into our inheritance, but it will not come without a repentant heart that is moved to action. This is what God is releasing on the earth in our generation. Father's transforming love and the heart of sonship—this is the message that the church and the world need to hear before the end comes.

Don't keep on living as an orphan in constant frustration, agitation, and fear—no love, no trust, no home, and no influence. What would your life be like if you had no fear? It would be like the life of Jesus, of whom Father said, *"This is My beloved Son, in whom I am well pleased."* Surrender your orphan heart for a heart of sonship. Enter the embrace of a Father who loves you more than you can possibly imagine. Hold close your identity as a son or daughter of the Father of Creation and explore it to your heart's content. Your inheritance is waiting for you. Don't let orphan thinking deny you what is rightfully yours as a fellow heir with

Christ. Be subject to Father's mission and experience life and peace, allowing Him to bring you into fruitfulness. Your family and the nations are waiting for you to enter into your inheritance!

QUESTIONS FOR DISCUSSION

WHO IS YOUR DADDY?

Part One

- Do you feel you have crossed the bar, of living from one storm to another and rarely finding a moment's peace, to being totally secure and at rest in God's love? Explain where you are on your journey to find home.

- What percent of the time do you feel you are subject to God's mission, and what percent of the time are you subject to your own?

- What is preventing you from making God's mission— receiving His love and giving it away—the top priority of your life?

- Have you taken the first step of accepting Jesus Christ as your Savior, or do you feel you need to make that decision today?

Part Two

- In what ways do you feel you have placed your work, ministry, or hobbies above intimacy with your spouse, children, parents, or others?

- Describe one way that the fear of trusting, fear of rejection, or fear of submitting to God's love has hindered intimacy (in-to-me-see) within the last week with one or more of your family members?

- What one thing can you begin surrendering to God this week in order to allow His love to begin displacing your independence or fear of intimacy? What steps can you take to do so? Would you want one of the people in your small group to help hold you accountable in an area this week?

Part Three

- What memories come to mind during the time you first began closing your heart off from a mother or father? What emotions were you experiencing? How did you feel at that time?

- Would you pray a prayer right now to forgive a mother or father for their inability to nurture, comfort, affirm, or protect you?

- Do you close your heart today to people you feel are not honoring or agreeing with you? If so, describe what you are feeling inside and how you respond to them.

• What counterfeit affections (possessions, passions, position, people, places, or power) have you struggled with in your search for comfort, acceptance, affirmation, and value?

Part Four

• Talk about a time when God placed someone in your life to be a mentor or confidant to you, but your orphan thinking was not able to receive them. What do you think it has cost you or your family for you to have rejected that relationship?

• Whose son or daughter are you today? Not to your natural parents, but who do you look to that speaks admonition and correction into your life and relationships?

• If you cannot think of anyone, what do you think is the root reason within you as to why there is no one in your life to help you personally (one-on-one) to grow and mature?

• Would you be willing to allow someone to begin mentoring you in your Christian walk and relationships? If so, who do you think is mature enough for you to respect and to receive admonition from?

Part Five

• Do you feel like a servant or slave who gets up each morning wondering what you have to do to please the master today? Or do you feel like a son or daughter who arises each morning feeling fully loved and accepted in the Father and who can't wait to give His love away to the next person you meet? Describe why you feel that way?

- Are you able to honor a "big fish" (those who have power to benefit you) but have great difficulty honoring "little fish" (those who cannot benefit you)?

- Within the last week, what ways have you bestowed gifts of honor upon a little fish? What was their response?

- What three little fish do you know who are in great need of feeling valued and affirmed by somebody? What can you do within the next week to bestow a gift of honor upon them?

Part Six

- Ephesians 6:2-3 tells us that when we honor our parents in a specific area of their lives, that area of life will also go well for us. Conversely, when we do not honor a certain area of their lives, it will not go well for us in that area. What destructive patterns have you seen in your parents that you now see at work in your life or relationships?

- Have you said to yourself, "I'll never raise my children the way my parents raised me"? In your parenting or as a spouse, are you reproducing those areas in your own life, in spite of any declarations that you've made? If so, in what way?

- Do you see areas in your life where you have brought hurt, disappointment, or wounding to one of your parents? Have you asked them for forgiveness (practiced the ministry of restitution) without seeking to blame them for your actions because of their negative behavior?

- Is your heart open to your mother or father? Or has it remained closed, rejecting them before they can reject you, thus seeking to protect yourself from further hurt or disappointment?

Part Seven

- Hebrews 13:17 tells us that if our leaders cannot think of us with joy, it is not profitable for us. When your name comes to your employer's mind, does he think positive thoughts of you because of the integrity, loyalty, and service that you have given to the company? If not, why do you think that is?

- Would your pastoral leaders think of you with joy for the heart of service and commitment that you have in your local church? If not, why do you think that is?

- What changes can you begin to make this week that will begin to sow loyalty and integrity toward authority?

- Do you think you need to go to one of your authorities and practice the ministry of restitution with them?

Part Eight

- Discuss the area of your thought life that tends to drag you down the most. What areas of your thoughts are most often in agreement with orphan thinking? What is preventing you from displacing those thoughts with thoughts of God's love toward you?

- Who put up with you during your years of "teenage thinking"—when you valued others for what they could do for you and not for relationship? Talk about your relationship with them and what they have meant to your life through the years.

- Who helped you mature and grow spiritually? What have these people meant to your life? Do they know how much you have valued their input? Do you need to apologize to them for anything? Do you think you should write a letter of thanks and appreciation to them for all they have sown into your life?

- What three ways can you express gratitude and honor to them over the next three months for what they have poured into you? How can you make what is important to them important to you?

APPENDIX A

Contrasting the Orphan Heart with the Heart of Sonship

Orphan Heart   Heart of Sonship

Orphan Heart		Heart of Sonship
See God as Master	IMAGE OF GOD	See God as a Loving Father
Independent/Self-reliant	DEPENDENCY	Interdependent/ Acknowedges Need
Live by the Love of Law	THEOLOGY	Live by the Law of Love
Insecure/Lack Peace	SECURITY	Rest and Peace
Strive for the praise, approval, and acceptance of people.	NEED FOR APPROVAL	Totally accepted in God's love and justified by grace.
A need for personal achievement as you seek to impress God and others, or no motivation to serve at all.	MOTIVE FOR SERVICE	Service that is motivated by a deep gratitude for being unconditionally loved and accepted by God.
Duty and earning God's favor or no motivation at all.	MOTIVE BEHIND CHRISTIAN DISCIPLINES	Pleasure and Delight
"Must" be holy to have God's favor, thus increasing a sense of shame and guilt	MOTIVATION FOR PURITY	"Want to" be holy; do not want anything to hinder intimate relationship with God.
Self-rejection from comparing yourself to others.	SELF-IMAGE	Positive and affirmed because you know you have such value to God.
Seek comfort in counterfeit affections: addictions, compulsions, escapism, busy-ness, hyper-religious activity.	SOURCE OF COMFORT	Seek times of quietness and solitude to rest in the Father's presence and love.

Contrasting the Orphan Heart with the Heart of Sonship
Continued

Orphan Heart   Heart of Sonship

Orphan Heart		Heart of Sonship
Competition, rivalry, and jealousy toward others' success and position.	PEER RELATIONSHIPS	Humility and unity as you value others and are able to rejoice in their blessings and success.
Accusation and exposure in order to make yourself look good by making others look bad.	HANDLING OTHERS' FAULTS	Love covers as you seek to restore others in a spirit of love and gentleness.
See authority as a source of pain; distrustful toward them and lack a heart attitude of submission.	VIEW OF AUTHORITY	Respectful, honoring: you see them as ministers of God for good in your life.
Difficulty receiving admonition; you must be right so you easily get your feelings hurt and close your spirit to discipline.	VIEW OF ADMONITION	See the receiving of admonition as a blessing and need in your life so that your faults and weaknesses are esposed and put to death
Guarded and conditional; based upon others' performance as you seek to get your own needs met.	EXPRESSION OF LOVE	Open, patient, and affectionate as you lay your life and agendas down in order to meet the needs of others.
Conditional and Distant	SENSE OF GOD'S PRESENCE	Close and Intimate
Bondage	CONDITION	Liberty
Feel like a Servant/Slave	POSITION	Feel like a Son/Daughter
Spiritual ambition; the earnest desire for some spiritual achievement and distinction and the willingness to strive for it; a desire to be seen and counted among the mature.	VISION	To daily experience the Father's unconditional love and acceptance and then be sent as a representative of His love to family and others.
Fight for what you can get!	FUTURE	Sonship releases your inheritance!

THE MINISTRY OF RESTITUTION

If our actions or attitudes have brought hurt to another person, there may be a need to go to that person and make right any wrong to break the destructive patterns in our relationships. Although God forgives us for each specific wrong the first time we ask, we may continue to reap what we have sown; so, in order to break that cycle and begin restoring trust, it is often necessary to make every effort to bring healing to others and to seek to restore the fractured relationship. Even if we feel the other person is 98 percent wrong and we are only 2 percent wrong, we are 100 percent responsible to walk in forgiveness and repentance for our 2 percent (see Matt. 5:22-26).

It may not be enough for another person to forgive you. You may still carry unconscious guilt or shame for the offense and have a need to ask for forgiveness to be free. There can also be a block in the relationship until you acknowledge to them that you have wronged them. The other person may have forgiven you, but trust has been violated. Until you acknowledge your offense, it is difficult for them to trust you again because forgiveness and trust are two different things. You will then either respond with self pity (feelings of sorrow over our suffering) or repentance in action that begins to rebuild trust with those who were offended (see 2 Cor. 7:9-11).

Self-pity seldom leads to transformed behavior or restored relationships.

- It diminishes, in our eyes, the gravity of each sin we commit against love and honor toward others.

- It hinders godly repentance when we feel that life has not been fair with us and believe that others are the cause of our frustrations. Thus we do not look to God but people to meet our need.

- It places the primary fault upon others for relational conflicts because we feel that we have been treated unfairly. *If they would not have done that to me…or…If only they would have done this for me, then life would be better and I would not be forced to act in such a way!*

- It excuses our negative attitudes by seeing the weaknesses in others and feeling that our rightness justifies our judgmentalism or actions.

- It attempts to persuade others to feel sorry for us and to acknowledge that we have been treated unfairly (defilement) thus strengthening the stronghold of self-pity within.

- It may try to compensate for our relational failures with increased hyper-religious activity, aggressively striving to earn self-worth or acceptance, or we may take on a false sense of responsibility and place all the blame upon ourselves for relational conflicts thus denying others the opportunity to deal with their own issues.

- It often leads to others feeling manipulated or demeaned by closing our heart to those who will not come into agreement with our self-pity, thus leaving others feeling that they have little value or honor in our presence.

- It may result in hidden anger at our feelings of loss or unmet expectations. This increases our blame toward others and results in deeper feelings of anger, insecurity, shame, isolation, apathy, self-condemnation, addictive compulsive behavior, and/or depression.

- It leaves us dissatisfied at work, church, and at home, and we want to escape to a place where we can find rest.

On the other hand, *godly repentance* always involves action. It is not just emotions and tears.

- It is to be so grieved at the wounding and stress our actions and attitudes have brought to others that we are now willing to humble ourselves and do whatever it takes to restore healthy relationships.

- It comes to hate the destructive habit patterns that have misrepresented God's love and grace to others.

- It becomes more concerned with others' needs than our own pride and walls of self-protection.

- It is willing to lay down the need to be right in order to see healing in those whom we have hurt or offended.

- It chooses to walk in openness and transparency, and willingly comes forward and acknowledges our sin against love and how we have hurt or offended others.

- It does not seek to make excuses, seek to put the blame on others, or diminish the depth of our self-deception or fear of intimacy with which we have struggled.

- It takes the focus off ourselves (self-pity) and begins to focus our energy upon humility, confession, forgiveness, repentance, and healing the pain that we have caused others.

Practicing the Ministry of Restitution

1. *Ask God to reveal to you each way you have brought hurt or offense to another person* (see Ps. 139:23-24).

- What is the basic offense? How did you demean, devalue, dishonor, or hurt that person?

- Ask the Holy Spirit to bring conviction and repentance to each individual issue (see Rom. 2:4).

2. *Ask mature spiritual leaders who know you personally to speak admonition into your blind spots.*

- Review with them the offenses that you have noted (see James 5:16; Eph. 4:15).

- Give them permission to speak the truth in love to you, about what they have seen in you that could be perceived as offensive or defiling.

- Ask for input as to how you can approach the offended person and bring restoration to the relationship.

3. *Ask forgiveness for how your immaturity, attitudes, actions, or neglect has caused hurt or offense.*

- Be thankful for this opportunity for growth. God is using this situation to help expose hidden destructive habit patterns and to bring them to death.

- Call on the phone to schedule a meeting with the offended party. A letter is not the best way because it does not give opportunity for them to respond, plus it documents instead of removes the offense. Approach them with humility and respect.

- Schedule the meeting during the best time of day for them. Allow plenty of time to discuss the issues.

- Begin the meeting by telling the person that God has been revealing to you how your attitude and actions have misrepresented God's love to them. Example: "God has brought to my attention how wrong I was (tell them the basic offense without going into detail). It would mean a lot to me if you would forgive me. Will you forgive me?"

- Do not go into too much detail, thereby giving the enemy something to work with and an opportunity to stir up bitterness, resentment, or defilement in the other person.

- Do not expect them to forgive you. They may, but do not require it, as it does not always happen.

- At this time, do not mention their faults. Just take ownership of your own. (Later, if your spiritual authority thinks it wise, and some trust is restored with the person, you may go to them about hurts you have received from them.)

- Do not try to diminish your offense by blame-shifting, justifying your behavior because of past hurts, or try to make an excuse because you were having a bad day. That only serves to diminish godly repentance. Take full ownership of your dishonor and misrepresentation of God's love.

- Ask the person if there are other areas they have personally seen that have brought offense to them or others. Ask forgiveness and apologize for each area they mention.

- You may want to do this individually with each family member you may have offended or defiled.

- If your attitudes or actions have brought offense or defilement to the whole family, workplace, or church, then after you have gone to them individually, you may want to gather the group together and ask them corporately to forgive you and to give you grace while you are attempting to make some changes in life.

4. *Ask the spiritually mature person, to whom you are accountable, to meet with you weekly or monthly.*

- Be sure that this individual is mature and is not afraid to speak the truth in love to you and that they do not come into agreement (defilement) with the issues you are having with others, but that they know how to help you judge yourself in each matter (see 1 Cor. 11:31).

- Discuss any other blind spots that are being exposed and have them pray with you over issues.

- Ask them how you can grow and mature relationally.

(A much more in-depth understanding of the importance of resolving conflicts is available in my CD audio series, "Would You Rather Be Right or Have Relationship?" Information on this subject can be found in the back of the book.)

EXPERIENCING FATHER'S EMBRACE

Experiencing Father's Embrace is an excellent resource for anyone interested in growing or ministering in the Father's love message. The author's style of writing makes this book easy to read, yet it is one of the most thorough and profoundly impacting books available on knowing God as a Father.

ISBN 0-7684-2348-1

HEALING THE HEART
OF THE FAMILY

(audio series)

As a Christian father and husband I ruled my family with control and intimidation. Trisha struggled with fear and permeable boundaries, and imparted insecurity and anger to our children. In this series we share the plan God revealed to us to bring healing in our family. We talk openly about how this brought love, unity, and reconciliation. Whether your children are 5 or 50 years old, the simple principles outlined here will help your family begin the process of healing and restoration.

BREAKING FREE

(audio or DVD series)

A teaching series that will identify why you do the things you don't want to do. *"The good that we wish to do we do not do, but we end up practicing the very evil that we do not wish to"* (Rom. 7). This teaching helps to identify the root causes of relationship conflicts and teaches how to crucify old habit patterns that have produced ongoing problems. This is one of Jack's most popular teachings.

FROM SLAVERY TO SONSHIP

(audio series)

Each of us is created with a capacity to receive love from a mother and father. Yet, many of us cannot say that we have behaved as true sons or daughters to our parents or to our spiritual fathers. When we rejected the "spirit of sonship" (a spirit of humility and yieldedness) as teenagers, we took on an attitude of independence or self-reliance, taking control of our lives. This can easily later overflow into our relationship with authority and Father God. This series addresses the issues of feeling like spiritual orphans (as if we have never had a safe or secure home), receiving our inheritance in Christ, and entering into true intimacy with God, spiritual authority, and others.

Shiloh Place Ministries
P.O. Box 5
Conway, SC 29528

Telephone: 843-365-8990
E-mail: info@shiloplace.org
Website: www.shiloplace.org